State Failure in the Modern World

State Failure in the Modern World

Zaryab Iqbal and Harvey Starr

Stanford Security Studies
An Imprint of Stanford University Press
Stanford, California

Stanford University Press
Stanford, California

Printed in the United States of America on acid-free, archival-quality paper

Library of Congress Cataloging-in-Publication Data

Iqbal, Zaryab, author.
  State failure in the modern world / Zaryab Iqbal and Harvey Starr.
       pages cm.
  Includes bibliographical references and index.
  ISBN 978-0-8047-7673-8 (cloth : alk. paper) — ISBN 978-0-8047-7674-5 (pbk. : alk. paper)

  1. Failed states.   I. Starr, Harvey, author.   II. Title.

  JC328.7.I73 2015
  321.09—dc23   2015010585

  ISBN 978-0-8047-9691-0 (electronic)

Typeset at Stanford University Press in 10/14 Minion

To Chris and Dianne

CONTENTS

Tables and Figures

TABLES

FIGURES

Acknowledgments

As with any project, a number of people have helped us along the way for whom we are most thankful. Between 2005 and 2010, we presented a series of papers that formed the basis for our project on state failure at the annual meetings of the Peace Science Society (International), the International Studies Association, and the American Political Science Association. Our thanks to all of those on the panels and in the audience who provided comments and feedback on our work. We would particularly like to thank Aydin Aysegul, Kristian Gleditsch, Ted Gurr, and James Lee Ray for their insightful comments as panel discussants. Harvey Starr would like to thank all those who commented on his presentations in 2008 at the Peace Research Institute of Oslo (PRIO), in 2009 at the Department of Political Science of the University at Buffalo, and at the Political Instability Task Force conference held in 2010. Starr owes particular gratitude to Glenn Palmer for urging him to edit a special issue of *Conflict Management and Peace Science* on "Failed States," which promoted interest in our project and in the study of failed states more generally. Zaryab Iqbal is grateful for the support she received from the Department of Political Science at Pennsylvania State University and the encouragement of her colleagues, particularly Donna Bahry and Scott Bennett. A very special thanks to Christopher Zorn for his constant support and his valuable input on all aspects of the project.

This book owes a tremendous debt to Geoffrey Burn of Stanford University Press, whose encouragement and patience were essential, and very much appreciated, in the publication of this manuscript. We also want to thank the anonymous referees for their insightful and encouraging comments and suggestions. Harvey Starr would like to acknowledge the support received from the University of South Carolina, especially a grant from the Magellan Scholars program and the assistance of Alex Severson. Zaryab Iqbal would also like to thank Andrew Martinez of Penn State for his assistance.

State Failure in the Modern World

1 Introduction

STATE FAILURE AND THE STUDY OF WORLD POLITICS

In the contemporary turbulent world of globalization and ever-increasing interdependence across individuals, groups, international organizations, and nation-states,[1] the existence of weak, fragile, or failed states is increasingly seen as a significant concern. In this book, we argue that state failure is associated with a range of factors pertaining to domestic politics as well as international influences, and that it is a phenomenon that is tremendously important to global security and human security in the current international system. More specifically, we demonstrate that the study of state failure, and assessing its impact on internal and international conflict and unrest, are consistent with a large body of international relations literature that engages the relationship between domestic and international politics—especially the study of civil war and development.

As the reader moves through this book, we hope that the strengths of our approach to state failure will become apparent. We provide a more nuanced theoretical analysis of state failure, along with an explicit discussion of its conceptualization, as well as the measurement of state collapse. Thus the book presents a unified conceptual and operational definition of state collapse, which is the foundation for a systematic empirical study of the set of collapsed states from 1946 to 2010. We do so using a multi-method approach, integrating comparative case studies with larger-scale quantitative analyses. The result is a comprehensive analysis of the full range of the failure process (from causes to duration to consequences), concluding with policy implications. These conclusions reflect empirical findings important for policy, including various factors underlying the onset of failure and its duration.

Because state failure is indeed an important issue in the global system, and one without simple answers, we need to set out the proper context for its study. This introductory chapter briefly situates the book amid the burgeoning literature on the importance of domestic political and social phenomena for international relations and foreign policy, as well as the need to "cross boundaries" between basic and applied research, between scholarly investigation and policy analysis (for example, Starr 2006).

The study of failed states would not have been found in the volumes filling the hypothetical library bookshelves dealing with international relations in either the pre–World War II or immediate postwar periods (for example, see Bobrow 1972). We will note why this is the case as we discuss the nature of state failure, outline the problems that exist in its study as well as suggest some remedies, and investigate a number of key questions about the causes and consequences of state failure. However, we must first look at and understand how a range of different scholars in political science as well as other disciplines, and especially in international relations and comparative politics, have come to the study of failed states—with their respective approaches, perspectives, and interests.

In the broad subfield of international relations, many students of conflict have moved to the study of civil war, particularly in the period after the Cold War. This was completely natural, as by that time it was quite evident that the primary arena of conflict in the contemporary world system had moved *within* states. Soon after the end of the Cold War, intrastate conflicts started emerging across the globe, whereas the incidence of interstate war rapidly declined. And thus students of international security and conflict processes came more and more to focus on internal violence—domestic strife, rebellion, revolution, and civil war—which more often than not would become internationalized in some way. It was equally natural for some of these scholars to become interested in the study of failed states, as most (but not all) of the cases of "failure" involved significant internal and/or internationalized conflict. In turn, the presence of conflict in failed states also accounts for an approach to the definitions, causes, and consequences of failed states that focuses on and stresses conflict; or at least starts with a concern about conflict. And we employ a similar approach to our exploration of state failure in this book.

A number of other scholars have come to the study of failed states through an interest in national or international security. Some of these have started their analytic journey with the broader concepts of "human development" or "human security," which begin to link both the conflict and political economy approaches to failed states by looking at the well-being of individuals and groups with a state.[2] Human development and human security approaches also serve as a gateway for the incorporation of issues of legitimacy, stability, and the political survival of leaders to the causes of state failure, and possible choices for policy alternatives.

Others in the IR subfield are interested in international political economy (IPE), while students of comparative politics are interested in comparative political economy (or CPE). They come at failed states from an interest in development, modernization, and the economic viability of the large number of states that achieved independence from colonial rule—starting the process with Ghana in 1957 and continuing throughout the 1960s and 1970s (and later). Recall that in the study of dependency-dependencia, and the set of debates that occurred in the 1960s and 1970s over the different models of dependency-dependencia, the point of contention was whether the main causative factors in these phenomena were internal or external. In the study of failed states there is a similar divide, with some political economy scholars who stress internal factors (such as poor governance, kleptocracy, different resource bases, reliance on single crops or resources, and so forth), and others who stress the global economic system, systemic economic hierarchies (for example, Wallerstein 1974), and predatory developed states that continue to pursue neocolonial dominance. We can find an analogous internal-external divide within the community of conflict scholars—those who focus on internal political, tribal/ethnic, separatist, and ideological factors and those who stress neighbors, regions, and the global system's geopolitical realities as causal factors in the nature, frequency, and intensity of both internal conflict and cross-border conflict. However, as with development and dependency, most scholars now understand that various combinations of *both* internal and external phenomena are needed to explain and analyze failed states.

Indeed, state failure is exemplary of the sort of contemporary political phenomena that "cross boundaries," and thereby require scholars (individually and in groups) to cross a variety of analytic boundaries as well (see, for example, Starr 2006 or Werner et al. 2003). It is exemplary in that the study of state failure involves "theories that posit complex causation, or multiple causal paths" (Braumoeller 2003, 209). In a number of ways, academic scholars have come late to the area of failed states, following the lead of international organizations and agencies (such as the World Bank), or the governments of the major aid-providing states (for example, the United States, Britain, Canada). This tardiness rests in part on the problems of crossing boundaries, or the unwillingness to do so. As Starr (2006, 1) has noted:

> Boundaries can indicate the limits of some set of phenomena; such simplification and specification can be valuable in the development of theory, concepts, and research design. However, boundaries too often loom as *barriers*, which can hinder how we think about phenomena, how we theorize about phenomena, and how we study the world about us. As scholars we must be conscious of artificial boundaries or barriers that constrain our thinking, and be just as conscious of finding ways to promote fertile theory and effective research design. In this sense we should think of the crossing boundaries approach *not* as some new theory or theoretical approach, but rather as a synthesizing device that helps us in organizing theory and research.

As a further example of crossing boundaries, we must also recognize another group of comparative politics scholars interested in state failure. These are Africa specialists who focus on sub-Saharan Africa. They also moved to the study of state failure because that region contains the largest concentration of weak, fragile, failing, failed, or collapsed states. For regional specialists, the two major approaches to state failure—conflict and economics/development—were often merged with a knowledge of local and regional tribal/ethnic relations. Their presence and contributions highlight the methodological dimension of crossing boundaries (including the combination of both quantitative and qualitative modes of analysis), as well as the need to cross the theoretical-empirical boundary to policy advice and evaluation.

The present authors' own interests in failed states stem from two of these approaches. One of the authors, with a longtime interest in geo-political and spatial factors in international relations, especially as related to conflict, was struck by an article in the March 5, 2005, issue of *The Economist*, "From Chaos, Order," which was about state failure. The consideration given to "low-income countries under stress" (LICUS) by the World Bank, and by the British government's Department for International Development (DFID) to "fragile states" had caught the attention of *The Economist*. *The Economist* (2005, 45) noted: "The chief reason why the world should worry about state failure is that it is contagious." If, as was argued, the extent and effects of state failure were key factors in understanding the global politics of the twenty-first century, then this argument had to be investigated through the lens of diffusion. The other author, who also has interests in the study of conflict, additionally has focused primarily on "human security"—an area concerned more with the security of populations than states. She has investigated a major component of human security—the relationship between violent conflict and the health and well-being of populations. In *War and the Health of Nations* (2010), Iqbal empirically demonstrated that the health of populations was an important consequence of armed conflict. As such, the idea that state failure, with all its possible negative consequences, could spread through spatial contagion was also of great interest. Both of the authors then, with different emphases, have had research programs in which a major component of that research addressed the *consequences* of war and violent armed conflict. An important consequence of conflict is further conflict—whether elsewhere in the system or repeated conflict by the same actors (see, for example, Most and Starr 1980).

However, as we moved to develop a design to study the diffusion of state failure and its effects, we encountered several fundamental problems. First, we found that a variety of definitions as well as a broad range of indicators of "failure" or "fragility" have been utilized in extant literature. Second, these identification exercises have been quite incomplete in their *conceptualization* of "failed states" or "fragile states" or "state failure." And third, not only have these treatments been incomplete, but they are highly problematic in that they have been essentially circular in their linking of concepts and measures, thereby creating considerable difficulties in research design. Thus, before we could move on to diffusion/contagion analyses, we found we had to address conceptualization and measurement issues as well as addressing the factors or conditions that increase the probability that a state will "fail."

We thus found ourselves engaging in a broad critique of the study of failed states, a natural step in promoting cumulation in an area of investigation. While questions of conceptualization and definition will be addressed below, and in depth in Chapter Two, we decided (as noted above) to deal with many of the conceptual problems by focusing our study on "state collapse." We think this approach complements that of others who critique a standard "state failure paradigm": for example, Charles Call (2011), who examines the failure of policy that does not deal with the specific factors (or, in his work, "gaps") relevant to any individual state. Starting with our conceptualization in the next chapter, our strategy of matching case studies in Chapter Five, and using our approach and findings in regard to policy in Chapter Seven, we believe that we have found a pathway to deal with such critiques.

THE APPEARANCE OF STATE FAILURE IN
THE POST–WORLD WAR II INTERNATIONAL SYSTEM

Why does the phenomenon of state failure now seem so prevalent? The number of states in the international system has roughly quadrupled since the end of World War II. With the dismantling of the Western colonial empires, the large number of artificial national entities created by colonialism became independent, joining the global system through membership in the United Nations as sovereign states. Most of these new states remained poor, weak, or unstable, reflecting their colonial heritage as well as other internal and external factors.

At the same time, these states emerged into an international system that was in the process of creating more and more constraints on the use of military power. As discussed in depth by scholars such as John Mueller (for example, 1989, 1995, 2011), a number of other circumstances acting to reduce the utility and practice of state-to-state violence and conquest took effect. The creation of postwar liberal institutions, both economic and political, with the UN Charter and attendant international law in the lead, along with the growth of the number of democracies in the international system, generated strong norms against the aggressive use of force and conquest.[3] While the power of the norm against the aggressive use of force to take territory has been used to help understand the lack of support in the General Assembly for Argentina after its attack on the Falklands/Malvinas (for example, see Franck 1985), it is perhaps best illustrated by the First Gulf War to prevent the Iraqi absorption of Kuwait. Mueller's argument for the "obsolescence of war," or Zacher's idea (2001) of the "territorial integrity norm" thus also meant that the newly independent and weak postcolonial states would be spared the possibility of being taken over by neighbors, or become part of multinational empires. We find few, if any, "failed states" in pre–World War II Western history, because they would simply have been swallowed by more powerful neighbors or imperial powers. Failed states appear only after the surge of independence in the 1960s and 1970s because the growth and spread of liberal norms have prevented the conquest or disappearance of weak states, as well as promoted efforts to keep them afloat (see Helman and Ratner 1992–93). All of these "territorial integrity" factors have been magnified in the post–Cold War global environment. Although weak or failed states exhibit what Krasner (2004) calls "failure of conventional sovereignty," an inability to meet the requirements of "conventional sovereignty" has not led to their actual demise.

Thus, it is clear that state failure is a post–World War II phenomenon, but also one that has been recognized for several decades. To take but one example, in 1994, the U.S. government established a State Failure Task Force (SFTF) (now called the Political Instability Task Force—PITF) to study the causes of state collapse. An equal amount of attention has been paid to the issue of state failure by nonstate actors. For example, the July/August 2005 issue of *Foreign Policy* presented the results of a study by the Fund for Peace (under the Carnegie Endowment for International Peace) that ranked states on a variety of indicators of instability. That study also cites the conclusion of the 2002 U.S. National Security Strategy that "America is now threatened less by conquering states than we are by failing ones." This warning was repeated by Secretary of Defense Robert M. Gates in a 2010 *Foreign Affairs* article: "In the decades to come, the most lethal threats to the United States' safety and security—a city poisoned or reduced to rubble by a terrorist attack—are likely to emanate from states that cannot adequately govern themselves or secure their own territory. Dealing with such fractured or failing states is, in many ways, the main security challenge of our time." Other diplomatic warnings were raised by Kofi Annan, that "ignoring failed states creates problems that sometimes come back to bite us," or Jacques Chirac, who warned of the threat failed states carry for the world's equilibrium.

Scholars have picked up on the threats that failed states might pose for international order and development as well. For example, it is in the context of weak/fragile/failed states that Mueller (2004) emphasizes the need for "policing the remnants of war." Mueller calls for developed states to contribute/devote disciplined police and military forces in order to promote peace, order, and good government in fragile or collapsed areas. Similarly, Rotberg (2002) warns of the linkages between state failure and terrorism, and stresses the importance of preventing state failure rather than reconstructing states after collapse. And, of course, as part of the human security approach, these states have been seen as having a wide range of negative effects on their own people as well as their neighbors, their regions, and the global community. One important theoretical reason, then, for studying state failure is the potential for the negative consequences of state failure—as well as state failure itself—to diffuse across neighborhoods or regions. Patrick (2006, 27) sums up this view of state failure in the global system: "It has become a common claim that the gravest dangers to U.S. and world security are no longer military threats from rival great powers, but rather transnational threats emanating from the world's most poorly governed countries."

PROBLEMS AND ISSUES

While the issue of state failure is clearly an important one in the contemporary global system and of concern to policy-makers, IGOs, NGOs, as well as academics, there exist substantial problems in the study of failed states. There is, in much of the literature, confusion over the meaning and nature of state failure caused by weaknesses in conceptualization and measurement. These weaknesses, in turn, lead to problems in research design and the meaning of the findings generated by that research.

Some of the problems stem from a point noted above—that the initial interest in state failure came from national governments or international organizations, and was addressed as a policy problem. In an article originally published in the Winter 1992–93 issue of *Foreign Policy*, Helman and Ratner described the failed nation-state as a "disturbing new phenomenon" and discussed the approach of the international community to such crises, particularly the role of the United Nations. While the governmental and IGO reports on issues related to state failure are very useful in highlighting this problem as a threat to domestic and international security, and the importance of preventing these catastrophic crises, most did not engage in social scientific analyses of the dynamics of state failure. For instance, most of these government or IGO sponsored studies did not clearly define state failure; a number seemed to conflate the concepts of state failure, regime instability, nondemocratic regimes, political violence, and civil wars.

Despite some very useful contributions from a variety of sources, the current literature on state failure is still characterized by a significant lacuna in terms of rigorous empirical analyses that evaluate state failure in a cross-national context. An initial endeavor toward filling this gap in the scholarly literature on state failure was a special issue of the journal *Conflict Management and Peace Science* (Starr 2008a). The articles in that issue assess questions related to the causes of state failure (Goldstone 2008), collapse of political order in Africa (Bates 2008), regional dispersion of the effects of state failure (Iqbal and Starr 2008), states' recovery from collapse (Chauvet and Collier 2008), and aid allocation to fragile states (Carment et al. 2008). Although these pieces make a valuable contribution to the understanding of state failure, the current book is better designed to explore the various dimensions of state collapse in a systematic fashion. And, while the existing literature is helpful in informing the theoretical direction of our project, this book is the first empirical study of state failure, which utilizes a broad spatial and temporal domain for statistical analyses. Therefore, we see this book as extending the literature on state failure by moving beyond descriptive examinations and providing rigorous analyses of the study of the causes and consequences of state collapse.

It is important to note that state failure as a concept is distinct from civil war. There is, in fact, a quite large and significant body of empirical literature on civil wars that we have consulted liberally in designing our models. Although we take into account the relationship between civil war and state collapse (and similarly, the relationship between economic development and state collapse), we focus on state failure as our dependent variable and aim to provide models to understand this specific phenomenon.

The next chapter is titled "State Failure: Conceptualization and Definition," and addresses definitional and conceptual issues in the study of state failure, clarifying the concept for the purposes of the analyses in the book. In this chapter, we review various measures of state failure used in academic and policy literatures, outline the problems of conceptualization and measurement in the study of state collapse, and introduce a definition and measure that solves these problems.

In Chapter Three, "Why Do States Collapse? Determinants of State Failure," we set forth our theoretical expectations regarding the causes of state failure, and empirically analyze the social, political, and institutional correlates of state collapse. We argue that state failure is determined by key social and political factors both at the domestic and international level. Specifically, using a sample of all states in the system from 1946 to 2010, we evaluate the influence of the type of governing institutions, states' involvement in civil and international armed conflict, various levels of domestic political turmoil, and economic development on the likelihood of state failure. Our analysis reveals that the risk of state failure is closely associated with armed conflict, domestic strife, and national income.

In Chapter Four, "The Duration of State Failure," we note that states that experienced a collapse of government during the time period we study remained "failed" for different lengths of time. While a majority of states recovered from collapse within a year, some remained in a state of failure for five or six years, and a few were unable to reinstate governing institutions for up to fifteen years. Drawing on the insights from our analysis of the determinants of the onset of state failure, we turn in this chapter to assessing the factors that influence the length of state collapse. The phenomenon of interest is the number of years it took these states to recover from collapse. Our preliminary findings suggest the primacy of economic factors in both extending and shortening the episodes of state failure. States that begin failure with higher levels of GDP (that is, higher levels of wealth and development) will take longer to recover. However, such effects are countered by the effects of economic openness in reducing the duration of the period of failure. In brief, we find that the factors so prominent in understanding the nature and cause of state failure are not the same as those relating to the duration of state failure and recovery from that condition.

The analyses of Chapter Four lead directly to Chapter Five, "Recurrent Collapse and Its Causes." Here, we turn to the question of why some states that fail achieve a lasting recovery, while others experience a recurrence of failure. We focus on the four cases of recurrent state failure found in our data set. In order to assess the factors that caused these states to fail twice, we undertake a series of four comparative case studies, comparing each of these four states with similar states that experience only a single failure during this period. This comparison is designed to offer insights into the specific factors that lead to recurrent failure in some states. We adopt a similar-systems approach, comparing states that are most similar to each other on a number of relevant dimensions. The motivation behind this choice of research design is that if similar states were able to avoid recurrent collapse, why did these four states fall prey to a second collapse? Keeping in mind that the four pairs of cases have already been matched on a number of factors, and the findings from Chapter Four, what does the context and history of collapse in each of the countries tell us that could help to distinguish the cases with two different outcomes: single-collapse states versus repeat-collapse states? With the use of comparative case analyses in this chapter, we bring the power of multiple methods to bear, complementing the systematic quantitative analyses of earlier chapters.

While Chapter Five investigates the consequences of failure in terms of recurrence, Chapter Six looks at "The Consequences of State Failure" with respect to how such effects might diffuse to contiguous neighbors or the failed state's region. In this chapter, we assess the negative effects of state collapse, with particular attention to the spatial diffusion of those consequences. We argue that the instability, unrest, and civil war that increase the hazard of state collapse are not limited to the failed/collapsed state; states neighboring—or states located within close distance of—a failed state are also likely to experience subsequently higher levels of political instability, unrest, civil war, and interstate war. We also evaluate the likelihood of state failure itself diffusing to other states. Our analyses indicate several major points regarding the regional effects of state failure. First, we uncover strong evidence of spatial effects associated with collapsed states. Such collapsed states, which are generated by political instability and armed conflict, in turn generate subsequent unrest, instability, and militarized conflict in their neighbors and regions. The findings also indicate that the more "minor" possible consequences of state failure—political unrest and instability — spread to a lesser degree than more intense forms of violence—especially civil war. At the same time, state failure itself *does not* seem to be regionally contagious.

Chapter Seven brings us to the policy dimensions of this study: "State Failure: Prevention and Management." In this penultimate chapter, we discuss the policy implications of our analyses, both in terms of preventing state failure and as they relate to the management and recovery of collapsed states. Note that, in general, much of the analysis of state failure can be seen as an exercise in policy evaluation. Previous investigators and commentators have uniformly considered state failure a dangerous phenomenon, with dire consequences both locally and regionally. Working from this belief, policy prescriptions have focused on forestalling such negative consequences. However, before we can have much confidence in any policy prescriptions, a number of analytic tasks, such as those outlined above, must be undertaken. Our findings can be used to help survey the set of policy recommendations extant in the scholarly and policy literatures, and in selecting the most promising avenues of policy choice and implementation—especially in mitigating diffusion effects and in directing our attention to those states with the greatest hazard of collapse. With these analyses in hand, we can evaluate past policy and provide future policy prescriptions for both states and international organizations in light of our results. Our findings, especially from chapters Five and Six, have clear implications for policy issues related to political and economic development in terms of international organization intervention, foreign aid, development, and democracy.

In the concluding discussion, we revisit the importance of studying state failure and the place of this subject in international politics and security studies. We also identify key directions for future research on state failure.

2 State Failure: Conceptualization and Definition

INTRODUCTION

We have noted the growing academic interest in the determinants of state failure and an acute awareness across the international community of the need for dealing with a variety of issues related to instability, weakness, and governance in the contemporary state system. State governments, nongovernmental groups, and international organizations have all been actively engaged in identifying such states, designated as "failed," "failing," "weak," "fragile," and the like. However, these identification exercises have been incomplete and inadequate in their conceptualization of failed states and state failure.[1]

Thus, in this chapter we address definitional and conceptual issues in the study of state failure, and work to clarify the concept of state failure for the purposes of the analyses that will follow. We will discuss the diversity and, indeed, confusion pertaining to the exact meaning and nature of state failure in much of the extant literature, resulting from weaknesses in conceptualization and measurement. We also argue that the lack of definitional clarity, in turn, has led to problems in research design, and consequently in the meaning of the findings generated by that research. There is also, in general, a more fundamental conceptual flaw, in that many definitions use the results of the analyses (which are based on the independent variables) to describe the concept under investigation—that is, the dependent variable. In contrast, we adopt a primary definition of state failure focused on the complete collapse of state authority. One empirical measure, based on POLITY IV data (Marshall and Jaggers 2011), is both conceptually distinct and exogenously measured: POLITY's "-77" coding for states, which indicates collapse, anarchy, or "interregnum." This measure also allows us to distinguish state failure from "state death" (Fazal 2004) and external invasion or annexation (which more closely resemble POLITY's "-66" designation). Focusing on the failure of states as viable sovereign entities allows us to distinguish collapsed states from states that are unstable, weak, or fragile. We argue that state fragility and failure are related but distinct phenomena, and offer definitional and measurement clarity (based on a model that distinguishes "failure" as an endpoint from failure as a process) in order to develop more effective research design. We outline a number of existing definitions of state failure below, as well as offer a solution to the problem of circularity in research using these definitions (and measurements).

In this chapter, we will start by reviewing various measures of state failure used in both academic and policy literatures,[2] outline the problems of conceptualization and measurement in the study of state collapse, and introduce a definition and measure that solves these problems. At the heart of these conceptualization and measurement issues is the diversity of purposes across existing studies and the definitions of state failure used in those studies. Some analysts start at the most basic level, with the role, nature, and capacity of states under the Westphalian ideal of sovereignty (as well as "conventional sovereignty" and its alternatives; see Krasner 2004), and the legal status of entities that might not approximate that ideal (for example, Grant 2004). But most who study failed states begin with some clear problem or set of problems that lead to a conclusion that a state has "failed." Some analysts focus on the loss of governmental control, which is heavily involved with conflict, both internal and external, while others focus on the inability of states to deal with societal conditions, especially those of extreme poverty. In state failure we have a very messy, contested concept in that it brings together the broad international relations subfield of conflict analysis with the equally broad subfield (which straddles international relations and comparative politics) of political economy. We not only have a concern with conflict—its causes, consequences, and management—but also with economic (and political) development. Both international conflict and IPE have large gaps and questions that defy broad generalizations. For example: why are some conflict rivalries enduring? Why are protracted social conflicts so impervious to many standard conflict management techniques?[3] What is the path (or paths) to economic development? Why do poor countries stay poor? Why can't we do better with economic aid? As such, it may be that the subject of state failure is best approached not from broad generalization, but Most and Starr's notion (1989) of sometimes true, *domain specific* "nice laws."[4]

The diversity of purposes has other dimensions as well. Some analysts want to dig into the phenomenon and fully understand the causes of state failure, while others want more fully to understand the consequences of state failure. Because state failure has negative consequences not only for the country involved but also for its contiguous neighbors, its region, and the global system as a whole, others want to develop early warning systems to alert policy-makers to impending failures, and thus trigger actions to stabilize unstable countries. Other analysts wish to discover ways to reverse failure, and generate "turnarounds" to bring failed states back to some measure of good governance. As we will elaborate below, there are also diverse purposes in regard to basic and applied research, and even the very nature of state failure as a process or an endpoint.

The two main dimensions of state failure identified in previous studies broadly fall into conditions of conflict and economic development, areas where scholars are involved in significant and growing amounts of research that cross levels of analysis. One purpose of our study is to *clarify* these dimensions of state failure and *separate* them from definitions of state failure. There exist a variety of definitions (and correspondingly, of indicators) of state failure or fragility, but these identification exercises have been quite incomplete in their conceptualization of failed states or fragile states or state failure. As noted, not only have these treatments been incomplete, but most are highly problematic in that they have been essentially circular in their linking of concepts and measures, thereby creating considerable difficulties in research design.[5] As we discuss below, most existing measures or indices of state failure incorporate a number of factors that may, in fact, be determinants of state collapse, such as civil strife and poverty. This leads to endogeneity issues that make it a challenge to study state failure as a dependent variable.

DEFINITIONS AND MEASURES

Defining the Concept

As noted above, "There is no agreed list of fragile states .... People also disagree about what constitutes fragility and no state likes to be labeled as fragile by the international community" (Department for International Development 2005, 7). We begin by outlining a sample of existing definitions of the general phenomenon of state failure. Material in italics is highlighted to indicate the specific focus of each definition, thus permitting comparison of the different perspectives on state failure.

One prominent definition of state fragility is that developed by the UK Department for International Development (DFID). According to their definition, a fragile state is one in which "the government cannot or will not *deliver core functions to the majority of its people*, including the poor. The most important functions of the state *for poverty reduction* are territorial control, safety and security, capacity to manage public resources, delivery of basic services, and the ability to protect and support the ways in which the poorest people sustain themselves." This definition provides four broad categories of "indicative features of fragile states": state authority for safety and security; effective political power; economic management; and administrative capacity to deliver services. Each is categorized in terms of the "capacity" and the "willingness" to provide them. Contrast these "core functions" of territorial control and poverty reduction to Rotberg's hierarchy of goods (2003). He argues that *security is* at the top of the hierarchy—and that security needs to be supplied before there can be "essential" freedoms to participate in government. Thus, he has put democracy second in this hierarchy before other goods such as healthcare, education, and the infrastructure of commerce.

Equally broad is a definition used by the Defence R&D of Canada (DRDC), where failure is equated with instability and defined as "when a state experiences significant *deficiency in its ability or willingness to provide basic public goods and services to the vast majority of the population, the vast majority of the time*" (Hales and Miller 2010, 6).

A substantially different definition of fragility is provided by the World Bank. The World Bank presents the LICUS[6] countries as "fragile" countries "characterized by a debilitating combination of *weak governance, policies and institutions*, indicated by ranking among the lowest (<3.0) on the Country Policies and Institutional Performance Assessment (CPIA)." In 2011 the World Bank defined a "fragile situation" as having either: "a) a composite World Bank, African Development Bank and Asian Development Bank Country Policy and Institutional Assessment rating of 3.2 or less; or b) the presence of a United Nations and/or regional peace-keeping or peace-building mission (e.g. African Union, European Union, NATO), with the exclusion of border monitoring operations, during the past three years."[7]

The World Bank notes that "[a] definitive list of LICUS is impossible to draw up since LICUS-defining characteristics are a continuum .... However, there is a consensus for analytic and operational purposes that some countries' policies, institutions, and governance can be defined as exceptionally *weak when judged against the criterion of poverty reduction*, especially with respect to the management of economic policy, delivery of social services, and efficacy of government." Until 2006 the World Bank did not disclose an explicit presentation of the indicators used in the CPIA or how the score was produced. However, an analysis by the Bretton Woods Project[8] sets out the basic methodology as well as a major critique:

> The CPIA is made up of 16 indicators, covering four clusters: economic management, structural policies, policies for social inclusion and public sector management and institutions .... Each criterion is given a score on a scale from one to six. The ratings, undertaken since 1997, are prepared annually in all countries by Bank country teams and then subjected to a process of internal review. In 2000, the Bank began disclosing the ratings, but only in an aggregated format—countries were ranked and placed into one of five groups from best to worst, referred to as "quintiles." In 2004, after calls from both the board and an external review panel, Bank management agreed to make the detailed scores for the 2005 ranking available for low-income countries. The ranking is particularly important for low-income countries as it plays a central role in the Bank's allocation of grants and low-interest loans .... The secrecy surrounding the CPIA exercise explains why there is so little literature on the topic despite the crucial role it plays. Barry Herman, former senior official of the UN financing for development office, has highlighted the inability of the CPIA to discriminate between countries or over time. He concludes that the CPIA, together with other similar indicators, should claim to be "no more than windows into a partial and clouded picture of development."

Yet another definition of state failure is offered by the Fund for Peace, which states that a "state is failing when its government is *losing physical control of its territory* or *lacks a monopoly on the legitimate use of force*. Other symptoms of state failure include the erosion of authority to make collective decisions, an inability to provide reasonable public services, and the loss of capacity to interact in formal relations with other states as a full member of the international community." The Fund for Peace (2006) uses a list of twelve indicators to assess the stability level of states. The indicators used by the Fund for Peace to determine whether a state is failing include demographic pressures, refugees and displaced persons, group grievance, human flight, uneven development, economic decline, delegitimization of state, public services, human rights, security apparatus, factionalized elites, and external intervention. Finally, the report of the State Failure Task Force (now the PITF) asserts that "'[s]tate failure' refers to the *complete or partial collapse of state authority* .... Failed states have governments with little political ability to *impose the rule of law*" (King and Zeng 2001, 623).

Note that there are parallels in the ways that states, IGOs, and NGOs try to identify, define, and measure the "rule of law," as well as provide policy advice in helping to implement it. Unfortunately, "rule of law" has many of the same problems of multidimensionality and multiple definitions and measures found in the study of state failure.[9] Additionally, the version of the SFTF/PITF definition presented above has the problem found in the focus of many IGOS and NGOs, which identify a failed state with the presence or absence of at least some minimal level of democracy. Many autocratic governments (and some of the partially democratic "anocracies") function perfectly well, and with an "iron fist" of control over society, while scoring badly on many measures of the rule of law.

Initially, the State Failure Task Force collected data on 1,231 variables for 195 distinct countries between 1955 and 1998 (King and Zeng 2001, 655). According to the Task Force report (Esty et al. 1998, 27–38), "state failure" included: revolutionary wars; genocides and politicides; and adverse or disruptive regime transitions. This list reveals another problem touched on above—combining a number of different phenomena under the heading of state "failure" when some might indicate anything but a failed state. We can see this lumping together of disparate phenomena in Krasner's comment (2004, 85): "Many countries suffer under failed, weak, incompetent, or abusive national authority structures." It is important to note that Rummel (for example, 1994) has demonstrated that genocide or politicide or abusive government (what Rummel labels as "democide") is most prevalent and most deadly in the most highly autocratic states, and is minimal in democracies. We cannot, however, automatically associate genocide with a weak or failed government—indeed, it more often reflects a strong government, but one with goals and policies that are abhorrent to democratic values.[10]

The complexity and multidimensionality of the concept of state failure can be vividly illustrated by looking at the "Special Issue on Failed States" published in *Conflict Management and Peace Science*, and edited by one of the present authors (Starr 2008a). Each of the five articles in the issue comes at state failure in its own way—some quite strikingly different. The lead article, by Jack Goldstone (2008), outlines several different causal paths to state failure.[11] Drawing on his past work on revolution and civil war, as well as his participation on the State Failure Task Force, Goldstone argues the need to find a "middle ground" between the view that each state failure is unique and more general propositions about the causes of state failure. Goldstone presents five major pathways, or stylized scenarios, that "may combine in various sequences": escalation of communal group conflicts; state predation; regional or guerrilla rebellion; democratic collapse; and succession or reform crisis in authoritarian states.

While Goldstone identifies "effectiveness" and "legitimacy" as the factors underlying "stability," the article by Bates (2008) draws on his previous formal work to identify conditions necessary for "political order" in his investigation of why things fell apart in late-twentieth-century Africa. The basic explanatory framework used by Carment et al. (2008) to explain state "fragility" is ALC—autonomy, legitimacy, capacity. The article by Iqbal and Starr (2008) was an early version of Chapter Six in this book, looking at some of the consequences of state failure. Chauvet and Collier (2008), and Carment et al. (2008), are expressly policy oriented and directly address how to deal with state failure. Whereas Iqbal and Starr look at the political and security effects of state collapse, Chauvet and Collier look specifically at economic factors and effects within a policy context.

The articles in this special issue reflect the heterogeneity and confusion noted above in the definition and measurement regarding "state failure" or "failed states." In brief, Goldstone defines state failure in terms of "stability," while Bates is interested in "political order" (and the Westphalian notion of sovereignty that governments have a monopoly on the use of force on their territory). For Bates, "the mark of state failure is the government's loss of its monopoly over the means of coercion." Iqbal and Starr, after raising the issue of conceptual and definitional disarray, see state failure as "collapse," using the POLITY code of "the complete collapse of central political authority" (elaborated below). Chauvet and Collier are interested in "failing" states, based on "inadequate performance of socio-economic functions." Thus they study low-income countries with extremely weak economic policies, institutions, and governance (similar to the LICUS countries of the World Bank). Finally, Carment et al. are concerned with at-risk or fragile states, with "state fragility" as a central focus, even while they admit it is "an elusive concept." For them "fragile states lack the functional authority to provide basic security within their borders, the institutional capacity to provide basic social needs for their populations, and the political legitimacy to effectively represent their citizens at home and abroad."

Returning to our discussion above, this lack of agreement on definition derives from a broader disagreement on the conceptual phenomena to be investigated (both in regard to intension, or the characteristics to be included, and extension, or the country cases to be included in the definitional box). Some of this divergence in approach derives from a difference between basic and applied research. The former is focused primarily on explanations (or causes) for states that exist at some "fail*ed*" *endpoint or condition*, while the latter is more concerned with a *process* in which at-risk, fragile, or fail*ing* states find themselves. For such policy-oriented analysts the problem is to understand the process in order to know how to intervene effectively to slow, halt, or reverse it.

If this characterization approximates what is actually going on, then it is possible that there is less confusion than appears at first blush. It may simply be a matter of asking scholars to be much more clear and explicit as to their purposes, to their research goals and the object of study: states we think have failed, or those that are failing. Two obvious analogies come to mind. One analogy contrasts many studies in international relations with those in comparative politics, contrasting the study of countries deemed *to be* democracies to the study of the process of *democratization*. Perhaps the most appropriate analogy is to a literature that studied the flip side of state failure—the study of social integration by which groups of people came together to create larger or more extensive political units! The early study of international integration, based on broad models of integration developed by Karl Deutsch and Ernst Haas more than fifty years ago, was similarly beset by a confusion that rested on a debate over whether integration meant a process or an endpoint. Depending on one's theory and research question, state failure, as with the earlier study of integration, can be either or both. It is up to each research project to clarify its focus and purpose, and then present the specific conceptualization and measurement of failure with the same detail.

As an example of the analytic difficulties that this diversity and range of definitions and purposes produce, Patrick (2006, 29) notes the difference in simply the number of "failed" states identified by difference sources:

> There is no consensus on the precise number of weak and failing states. The Commission on Weak States and U.S. National Security estimates that there are between 50 and 60; the United Kingdom's Department for International Development classifies 46 nations with 870 million inhabitants as "fragile"; and the World Bank treats 30 countries as LICUS. These divergent estimates reflect differences in the criteria used to define state weakness, the indicators used to gauge it, and the relative weighting of various aspects of governance.

CONCEPTUAL AND METHODOLOGICAL CONSIDERATIONS

Lack of agreement about the concept, and lack of clarity as to purpose, are key problems in the failed state literature. There is also, in general, a more fundamental conceptual flaw, in that many of the projects/scholars present a definition that uses the results of the analyses (which are based on some set of independent variables) to describe the concept under investigation—the dependent variable. We can see from many of the definitions listed that the characterization of state failure used is based on specific factors or variables that are then used to help study the presence of failure or its causes. This is what we called circularity above, with problems of endogeneity that raise serious questions as to the validity of findings.

Each of these issues follows from problematic conceptualization processes. Following the arguments presented in Goertz's extensive investigation (2005) of social science concepts (as well as Adcock and Collier 2001), we find analysts focusing on indicators or data *before* dealing with the more important, and logically prior, levels of conceptualization. As Goertz argues, the "indicator/data" level of conceptualization should only come after scholars identify the "basic" level. For Goertz, the "basic" level is one that is "cognitively central" and identifies "the noun to which we attach adjectives" (Goertz 2005, 5). This is analogous to Adcock and Collier's "Level 1. Background Concept." For Adcock and Collier (2001, 531) this is the "broad constellation of meanings and understandings associated with a given concept" (see also Collier and Levitsky 1997). Adcock and Collier also see a feedback loop from the Background Concept *to* the task of Conceptualization, and then the task of Revisiting the Background Concept.

For Goertz, the next level is the "secondary" level of conceptualization, which involves providing the "constitutive dimensions of the basic level ...." The secondary-level dimensions form much of the ontological analysis of concepts" (Goertz 2005, 5). Adcock and Collier (2001, 95) call their Level 2 the "Systematized Concept," somewhat similar to Goertz but "a specific formulation of a concept used by a given scholar or group of scholars; commonly involves an explicit definition." That is, here Goertz's second level is applied for a particular approach and the dimensions that are relevant to that approach. It is only after performing these conceptual exercises that Adcock and Collier or Goertz move on to the development of indicators and how to score cases on these indicators.

For example, when examining the study of the democratic peace, Goertz stresses that theory should drive concepts and methodology. He argues that many scholars have wrongly moved directly to indicators or measures of democracy, and have ignored working from the first two levels (the "basic" and "secondary"). Most and Starr (1989) make the same argument in discussing the "research triad" of theory, logic, and research design. They note that scholars must identify *why* they want to study a certain concept (in their case, war), and *which of the dimensions or aspects* of that concept are important for the development of the specific research question the scholar wishes to pursue (very much like Adcock and Collier's Level 2). The conceptual components of the research enterprise are thus linked logically to the appropriate research design that needs to be developed to investigate the specific research question.

Considering the definitions and characterizations of state failure that we have noted, we believe that there is an analogously problematic conceptualization for "failed" states. Researchers must clearly understand the questions they want to ask, and *why*. Being explicit about these questions is central to the Most and Starr approach and what Adcock and Collier call the "Background Concept" and "Systemized Concept." Researchers must also recognize that, as a complex concept, "state failure" has a number of different dimensions: weakness, fragility, death, or our present focus on collapse. Above we noted the diversity of purpose in studying state failure in all of its various forms. In addition, note also that the different purposes that motivate analysts can then be linked to another important difference in views—state failure as either process or endpoint, and thus a view of the research that is either basic or applied.

Bottom line: because of the array of conceptual problems noted, some analysts have moved to listing "indicators" before considering a full conceptualization, as in the Goertz critique of data on democracy (in Adcock and Collier's terms, moving to Levels 3 and 4 before paying the needed attention to Levels 1 and 2). By so doing, some have also confused conceptual/definitional elements with descriptive elements, independent variables, operational indicators, and/ or causal factors. Our solution is to be clear in our conceptualization, dealing with these problems by adopting a primary definition of state failure that relies on complete collapse of state authority, which was elaborated above. We argue that focusing on the failure of states as viable sovereign entities in its most extreme form (and by looking at some of the worst cases) allows us to distinguish collapsed states from states that are unstable, weak, or fragile. We assert that state *fragility* and *failure* are related but distinct phenomena (or dimensions). Here we offer definitional clarity in order to develop more effective research design. States may be weak, or be fragile, or be autocratic, or be both autocratic and cruel to segments of their population, or be absorbed by other states—but not be "failed states" in regard to our use of "collapse." We now turn to our operationalization of state failure.

OPERATIONALIZING STATE FAILURE

The central problem identified above is the issue of circularity in the conceptualization of state failure. We avoid this problem by limiting our study to states with completely collapsed central governments, turning to the POLITY IV data (for example, Marshall and Jaggers 2011) to identify such states. The POLITY IV data famously provides "autocracy" and "democracy" scores for all country-years in the data set, with an "anocracy" category for countries with mixed scores between autocracy and democracy. The POLITY IV data have been widely used in the study of the democratic peace and other studies that require a democracy score for the state under analysis. In developing these scores, POLITY recognized there were country-years when it was not possible to place a country on the autocracy-democracy continuum. POLITY IV, therefore, also provides three "standardized authority" codes that are used to indicate the status of a state actor which would be different from the normal legal status of a "sovereign" state—that is, when a government representing the state exercises control over a territory and the people living on that territory.

Importantly, as noted, these codes were created for purposes quite different from the purposes of those studies which are specifically directed at state failure. The first of these standardized codes is called an "Interruption Period" (coded –66), and indicates when a country is occupied by a foreign power during a period of war. The second is a "Transition Period" (coded –88), which indicates a period before the creation of a new polity, particularly for democratic or "quasi-democratic" areas that will move, or are in the process of moving, to full independence. The third category is the one of interest to us. This is the set of countries labeled "Interregnum Periods" (coded –77). According to the POLITY IV *Dataset Users' Manual* (17–18): "A '-77' code for the POLITY component variables indicates periods of 'interregnum,' during which there is a *complete collapse of central political authority* .... Interregnal periods are equated with the collapse, or failure, of central state authority, whether or not that failure is followed by a radical transformation, or revolution, in the mode of governance" (emphasis added). As Fearon and Laitin (2009, 27) note in a report to the PITF: "As we understand it, the core intuition is that there are times when a country has no clear regime whose characteristics can be reliably coded. There is a 'collapse of central authority' and thus no regime to code." They go on to identify the key POLITY criteria for applying a –77 code: "How to code whether there is a coherent central government that can act as such? Implicitly, it seems that POLITY coders are now using the observation of (a) multiple, strong claimants to authority at the center, and (b) substantial violence among factions competing for power at the center, as the main criteria" (2009, 27).

These periods are distinct from periods of instability and/or war during which a state's governing institutions remain in place. Again, although instability or state weakness may be measured on a continuum, in our explicit conceptualization (and for our purposes) we view failure as an absolute, dichotomous condition; a state either fails or it doesn't. Clearly, in our research we are treating state failure as an "end point condition," as described above. We consider, therefore, only –77 countries to be failed. As noted above, other states, as long as they have a central government, are not considered to have experienced a failure or complete collapse—regardless of their levels of instability. This is not to minimize the importance of studying factors that make states weak or fragile, but to distinguish a complete collapse of state government from phenomena such as ineffective governance, political turmoil, rapid turnover of regimes, unstable institutions, or lack of democracy. State fragility may be associated with state failure but is not identical to it.

The POLITY data thus indicate observations not attached to any specific theory, model, or approach to state "failure" or "fragility." The –77 code, rather, is based on the disappearance of central political authority, which is directly relevant to our research question and our view of state failure as the collapse of a state (including authority/legitimacy and capability).[12] Most critically for our purposes, it is not derived from a list of factors that are used as both explanatory variables and also to operationalize the phenomenon to be explained. The –77 category *captures an intense and explicit view* of state failure: "a complete collapse of central political authority." It also provides us with an unambiguous set of units of analysis. The states selected for analysis are not simply "fragile," or those with a high probability of, or potential for, failure, or those identified only because they are experiencing a civil war.[13]

In sum, we have made a decision to use certain dimensions of the concept of "failure" as central to our study. Failure is seen as an endpoint. We require this view of failure to examine questions regarding the consequences of failure, such as recurrence or diffusion. We are concerned with the endpoint of "collapse." This is the conceptualization of state failure we use in this study. First, it equates "failure" with "collapse." Second, it is unambiguous by focusing on the "complete collapse" of central authority. Third, as noted above, it is an explicit view of failure in its most extreme form (recall that "collapse" is at the far end of Rotberg's continuum). Fourth, it does so without referring to any single factor, or set of factors, that must be or are most probably present to cause that collapse.

The −77 coding thus captures the idea of a state without a functioning government, incapable of providing order and carrying out the responsibilities that international law has always expected of states claiming sovereignty. Our dependent variable of "state failure" is then represented by those country-years coded as −77 in the POLITY data. Using the −77 code, we identify 26 failed states, 21 years that saw a first-collapse (with 33 collapses altogether), and a total of 121 country-years in the dataset from 1946 to 2010 that were coded −77. Four states failed twice during this period, and the remaining 22 states each failed once for varying periods of duration.

One exercise that can be conducted is a comparison of failed states generated by the POLITY −77 coding with other lists of fragile or failed states. We do this to illustrate that various definitional approaches are indeed measuring different dimensions of state vulnerability, and thus yield different research outcomes. Our proposed measure of state failure offers a more precise and unambiguous definition of the concept. With this view of state failure, and a set of states generated by the POLITY data, we can conduct some descriptive conceptualization comparisons (see Table 2.1). For each "failed" state in Table 2.1 (according to our POLITY-based indicator), we assessed how they measured against various definitions or characterizations noted above. We use four indices for comparison. First, we used the scores generated by the Fund for Peace, where the higher the score of the Failed States Index, the worse off the state was. That data, presented in July/August 2005, included the sixty states scoring highest on the index, with the Ivory Coast topping the list with a 105 index; the sixtieth ranking state was Gambia at 82.4. We also use the CPIA/LICUS index rating, which assigns each state a "grade" from A to F, with F standing for "failing."

We examined two other indices as well. Because at least some of the studies noted above are concerned with state capability and performance, especially with regard to poverty and quality of life, we have included the 2003 score on the World Bank's Human Development Index (HDI); the lower the HDI scores the worse off are the countries. In 2003, the average for all countries was 0.71, while that for the lowest-income countries was around 0.30. Finally, using data

TABLE 2.1: Illustrative Comparison of Definitions/Indices of State Failure

State name	Years since last failure	Fund for peace (1994)	Hobbes Index (1997)	HDI (2003)	CPIA/LICUS Index
Afghanistan	9	99	—	—	—
Angola	12	87.3	16.75	0.44	F
Bosnia-Herzegovina	10	93.5	62.06	0.78	B
Burundi	9	94.3	11.27	0.37	F
Chad	21	100.9	42.93	0.34	D
Comoros	9	—	40.15	0.54	F
Congo DR	5	105.3	13.16	0.38	D
Ethiopia PDR	13	91.1	39.11	0.36	C
Guinea Bissau	6	—	37.02	0.34	F
Cambodia	29	—	19.02	0.57	D
Laos	32	91.5	39.75	0.54	F
Lebanon	15	88.9	77.17	0.75	—
Lesotho	6	—	44.73	0.49	C
Liberia	9	99.5	—	—	—
Nicaragua	24	—	69.10	0.69	A
Sierra Leone	3	102.1	19.71	0.29	D
Somalia	3	102.3	—	—	—
Uganda	19	91.7	23.83	0.5	A
Zaire	3	—	13.16	—	—

provided by Bueno de Mesquita et al. (2003), we present the 1997 scores of each state using the Hobbes Index. This is a measure of the social welfare of a country's people, taking into account the dimensions of "misery" that represented Hobbes's view that life in the state of nature was "short, nasty, solitary, poor, and brutish" (Bueno de Mesquita et al., 2003, 461). This index includes the annual experience of a state with civil war, revolution, and international war, as measures of "brutishness." Demographic, health, social, and political measures were used to capture the other four elements. The Hobbes Index varies between zero and 100, with 100 indicating the best scores. Bueno de Mesquita et al. (2003) report that the average Hobbes Index for 1,865 country-years was 62.13 (463).

Table 2.1 is useful in that it confirms our observations about the study of failed states—and the mix of definitions, indicators, and units of analysis. As an illustration, we have compared the set of nineteen states coded –77 during the 1970–2000 period across their scores on other indexes. First, we see that some states fail more often than others and have differing periods of time since their last failure.[14] The range on the Hobbes Index is quite wide, with Burundi at a low of 11.27 but with Lebanon at 77.17 and Nicaragua at 69.10, both above average (and Bosnia at the average with 62.06). Five of the states listed receive an "F" on the CPIA/LICUS scale; another four receive a "D." However, two states receive an "A" and a third gets a "B." The thirteen states for which there are 1994

Fund for Peace scores all perform quite poorly. Reflecting the "less" and "least" developed status of most of these countries, the HDI scores are very low, with only Bosnia and Lebanon better than the world average. But, as Patrick (2006, 30) reminds us, we cannot focus only on "capacity" but must take "will" into account as well.

Most and Starr (1989) developed a "quick and dirty" short-cut approach to constructing simple experiments and hypothetical cases to see if a research design was on the right track. Using this strategy of "stylized facts" to compare how states rate on different schemes, on the face of it, it appears that these various indexes are indeed measuring different things. The impact of internal or external war is greater in some measures (or "conceptualizations") of failure/fragility, while poor economic performance is more important in others.

We can make the same point by flipping the argument around. One well-known and widely used measure, the Failed States Index of the Fund for Peace, is calculated from twelve social, economic, and political indicators. All of these indicators relate to aspects of state weakness or instability. Rank order correlations were run between the Failed States Index (2007) and three other indexes: the Brookings Institution State Weakness Index (using 2007 data, from Rice and Patrick 2003), the Global Peace Index (Vision of Humanity 2008), and 2006 HDI data. Because the Failed States Index was built out of measures related to the other indices, there are Spearman rank order correlations of 0.689, 0.604, and 0.534, respectively (all statistically significant). While the results indicate a general similarity across the measures, even here we see that the concept of failure has a number of dimensions. And while statistically significant and in the right direction, the rank order correlation between the Failed States Index and 2007 Freedom House data (which is coded across Free, Partially Free, and Non-Free categories) was only −0.332, indicating that democracy and failure are only weakly related.

The chapter that follows addresses the question of why states collapse and seeks to investigate the causes of state failure (collapse). Our theoretical expectations derive from the various lists of possible causes set out in the literature partially reviewed above. We have selected a short list of key independent variables that are suggested by these studies and others to assess which factors affect the hazard of state failure. Specifically, we evaluate the influence of the type of governing institutions, states' involvement in civil and international armed conflict, various levels of domestic political turmoil, and economic development on the likelihood of state failure. It is to these analyses we now turn.

3 Why Do States Collapse?
Determinants of State Failure

INTRODUCTION

As discussed in the previous chapter, it is clear that while the issue of state failure is certainly an important one in the contemporary global system and of concern to policy-makers, IGOs, NGOs, and academics, there exist substantial problems in the study of failed states. There is, in much of the literature, confusion over the meaning and nature of state failure, resulting from weaknesses in conceptualization and measurement (for example, see Starr 2008b). Chapter Two addressed the issue of definition in the study of state failure and offered a working definition for the concept, which we use in the analysis in this chapter to examine the determinants of state collapse. Our definition of state failure focuses on complete and utter collapse of a state's central authority; we use the terms "state failure" and "state collapse" interchangeably to reflect a total absence of a central government for a certain period of time. In light of this definition, we revisit some of the analyses assessing correlates and causes of state failure. The results highlight the central factors involved in state failure and provide new insights as well as added confidence to some findings of earlier studies. Thus, in this chapter, we evaluate the factors or conditions that increase the probability that a state will fail. Our analysis reveals that the risk of state failure is closely associated with states' involvement in armed conflict, domestic strife, and national income.

Policy analysts have seen failed states as being associated with a range of economic, social, political, and military problems. Additionally, they have been seen as having a wide range of negative consequences for their own people, their neighbors, their regions, and the global community. As discussed in the opening chapter, *The Economist* (2005, 45) notes simply that the chief reason why the world should worry about state failure is that it is contagious. One important theoretical reason, then, for studying state failure is the potential for the negative consequences of state failure—as well as state failure itself—to diffuse across neighborhoods or regions (an issue we take up in the next chapter). State failure as a phenomenon of political economy is also fully embedded within a set of theoretical contexts currently being employed by political scientists to study activities, relationships, and problems that cross the internal-external levels of analysis, as well as other analytical boundaries.

The two main dimensions of state failure identified in previous studies broadly fall into conditions of conflict and economic development, areas in which scholars are involved in significant and growing amounts of research that cross levels of analysis. One purpose of the analysis here is to *clarify* these dimensions of state failure and *separate* them from definitions of state failure, an exercise we consider necessary to establishing causality in the understanding of state collapse. A key factor in understanding the global politics of the twenty-first century is the extent and effect of such failure in the state system. One of our initial concerns was the likelihood of regional diffusion of the consequences of state failure. However, as noted, when we moved to develop a design to study diffusion and other effects of state failure, we encountered two fundamental problems. First, we found that there exists a wide range of definitions (and correspondingly, of indicators) of failure or fragility. Second, these identification exercises have been quite incomplete in their conceptualization of failed states or fragile states or state failure, which was the focus of Chapter Two. Not only have these treatments been incomplete, but all are highly problematic in that they have been essentially circular in their linking of concepts and measures, thereby creating considerable difficulties in research design. This leads to endogeneity issues that make it a challenge to study state failure as a dependent variable. Having addressed the issue of defining and measuring state failure we now move on to examining its correlates or determinants.

DETERMINANTS OF STATE FAILURE

Our operationalization of failed states provides us with a dependent variable that can adequately be evaluated through empirical analysis. The superiority of our measure lies in its independence from any likely influences on the incidence of state failure. Unlike the indices of state failure described above, our measure does not by construction include any factors—such as regime type, national income, or civil war—that may in fact be determinants of state collapse. We turn now to the question of what causes states to experience a complete collapse and thus fail as viable sovereign entities. Explicitly drawing upon the theory and findings of earlier work—from the projects noted above as well as other projects such as the one on fragile states supported by the Canadian International Development Agency (see, for example, Carment et al. 2006)—we argue that among significant determinants of state failure presented in that literature are levels of democracy, incidence of civil and international armed conflict, domestic unrest and instability, and national income.[1]

States that support stable democratic institutions enjoy higher levels of resilience to collapse. Democratic regimes, because of institutional strength as well as their broad public support, are less fragile and vulnerable to failure than states that lack strong democratic institutions.[2] At the same time, highly autocratic regimes also have an established authority structure and a strong central government. Thus autocratic regimes may be able to maintain domestic stability through extremely repressive measures and effective centralized control. In both established democracies and established autocracies, the domestic political institutions are likely to be more durable and powerful—hence a lower likelihood of state failure. In contrast, states that are transitioning from one kind of regime type to another (often moving through anocratic status) lack the institutional stability of either democracies or autocracies and are, therefore, more susceptible to collapse. Transition in either direction—toward or away from democracy—could render state institutions weak and prone to collapse. We thus expect a curvilinear relationship between democracy and the likelihood of state failure: states that are neither extremely repressive and autocratic nor established democracies are at the highest risk of collapse because of the lack of either stable democratic institutions or a strong central authority willing and able to repress any threats to the state. Arguments exist for such a curvilinear relationship between democracy and intrastate conflict (for example, Hegre et al. 2001; Sambanis 2002) as well as other indicators of political violence, such as terrorism (Eyerman 1998) and assassinations (Iqbal and Zorn 2007).

The most significant threat to the existence of states remains violent conflict, either civil or international. In fact, civil wars are believed to be so closely associated with state collapse that many of the definitions of state failure discussed above use civil wars to measure state collapse. In addition to reflecting deep-seated divisions and propensity for violence within a state, civil wars take a drastic toll on a society through their effect on population, infrastructure, economy, and political institutions. Civil wars are particularly devastating for a state because the fighting is not usually limited to border areas, and losses incurred by both sides have a detrimental effect on the country. In addition, civil wars are generally aimed at replacing a state's government, bringing about significant change in the political institutions, or separating a substantial portion of the territory/population into a new state through secession, all of which make states involved in domestic conflict particularly vulnerable to collapse.[3] Moreover, a large number of civil wars in the current international system are ethnic conflicts, with intense hatred and historical rivalries between the opposing sides; such conflicts have the potential to be exceptionally devastating.[4] It is, therefore, reasonable to expect a positive relationship between civil conflict and state collapse.

Although civil wars are particularly associated with state failure, international conflict may also result in the collapse of a state because of high levels of death and destruction. Whereas a border dispute or an interstate conflict with limited aims is unlikely to cause a belligerent state to fail, war aims of a foreign rival may include rendering the political institutions of a state ineffective or causing large-scale devastation of a society. A high-intensity international war may, thus, lead to state collapse. Wars are clearly associated with destabilization of state and societal institutions. However, a number of different phenomena pertaining to domestic political upheavals, but falling short of war, could also have destabilizing effects on a state and contribute to state failure. Occasions of political tumult range from minor instances of protest, such as antigovernment demonstrations, to all-out civil war. In order, therefore, to assess the influences on state failure adequately, it is important to take into account both wars and other indicators of political upheaval that might undermine the durability of state institutions. Actions that don't result in war—but may nonetheless destabilize a state—include strikes, riots, revolutions, government crises, coups, and guerrilla warfare. All of these phenomena may contribute in varying degrees to state collapse.

Wealth, on the other hand, is generally believed to reduce the likelihood of state failure. Here we argue that economic development is likely to have a strong negative relationship with state failure/collapse/fragility. This proposed relationship is consistent with extant arguments about the effects of economic development on the causes of civil war, and on the democratic peace. The work of Paul Collier and colleagues (for example, Collier and Hoeffler 2004), among others, indicates that wealth, growth, and development reduce the probability of civil war. Similarly, Fearon and Laitin (2003) argue that the risk of civil war is greatly diminished in economically developed countries, with wealth washing out the effects of ethnicity in weak states. Additionally, some investigations of the democratic peace have concluded that the democratic peace effects are most powerfully felt between democracies with developed economies, and may even be limited to economically developed democracies (for example, Mousseau 2000, 2003). In a similar fashion, we might expect that higher levels of national income and stable economies make states resilient to collapse. Moreover, there is a broad literature generated by economists and political scientists that links open markets and free trade to growth and development (see, for example, Olson 2000). If wealth, growth, and development reduce the probability of state failure, and open trade plays a major role in economic growth and development, then we may also propose that economic openness and higher levels of trade reduce the likelihood of state failure through an increase in prosperity as well as engagement in the international system.

Finally, we believe that the likelihood of state failure has increased in the post–Cold War era. During the Cold War, superpower interference in the domestic institutions and international interactions of states within their respective spheres of influence tended to depress the occurrence of state failure. In the absence of the direct and indirect support that was offered by the Cold War superpowers to regimes in various world regions, the probability of state collapse has increased.[5] One possible explanation for this is that during the Cold War the United States and its West European allies were both willing and able to provide the support to keep current or potential supporters stable. A good review of literature that supports this proposition is presented in Van de Walle (2004, 96). This argument is consistent with previous findings by Simon and Starr (1996, 2000). Developing a simulation that modeled state response to two-level internal and external threats to security, Simon and Starr (2000) demonstrate that "endangered democracies" which had neighbors that were already democratic could set the stage for the internal governmental extraction of resources—which could then be devoted to societal development. That is, "endangered" democracies may be able to recover security through attempts to "buy off" domestic threats rather than deter them, and by improving legitimacy with the allocation of resources to society (resources that did not have to be devoted to external security). Simon and Starr (2000) thus also show that ally support is crucial for new democracies facing internal threats. We suggest an analogous effect for the Cold War and the hazard of state failure.

In summary, our argument about the causes of state failure suggests that regime instability or transition, armed conflict, and various types of domestic political turmoil contribute to state failure; economic development and openness reduce the likelihood of state collapse.

DATA AND ANALYSIS

The dependent variable in our study is *State Failure*, which is represented by the assignment of a POLITY code of −77 to a country in a given year. In any given year, if a country does not experience failure, it is assigned a value of zero; a value of 1 is given to country-years with a state failure. In our data, 30 out of 161 countries experienced a complete collapse at least once during the period from 1945 to 2009. Some of these states were coded as failed for multiple country-years; for instance, by our definition Laos experienced twelve years of failure, and Lebanon fifteen such years.

Among the covariates is regime type of states in each year. Regime type is operationalized as POLITY IV scores for country-years. POLITY scores range from −10 to 10, with −10 representing the lowest level of democracy and 10 the highest.[6] Those states with a score of −10 are the most autocratic, while 10 represents the highest level of democracy. For reasons given above, we expect highly democratic states to be less likely to fail, but extremely repressive states may also be able to maintain stability—and thus avoid failure—by depriving their populations of any opportunities to protest or rebel. This implies that both highly democratic and highly autocratic states are less prone to failure than states that are either the anocratic "mixed" regimes or transitioning from one form of government to another. To test for a curvilinear relationship between democracy and state failure, we include a quadratic term for democracy. Both democracy variables are lagged to reduce the likelihood of endogeneity.

We include two independent variables to evaluate the effects of armed conflict. We measure the presence of *Civil War* in a country-year through a dichotomous variable: 1 if there is a civil war, zero otherwise. We also include a variable for the number of *External Conflicts* in which a state is involved in a given year in our data. The number of interstate conflicts in which states were involved in a year ranges from zero to six. The data for civil and international wars were acquired from the PRIO/Uppsala dataset on armed conflict (Strand et al. 2004). We expect both types of armed conflict to have a positive effect on state failure, although civil wars are likely to have a stronger positive relationship with state collapse because of their destabilizing effect on domestic governance.

To further assess the effect of domestic political tumult on a state's propensity to fail, we include two variables that measure phenomena of internal turmoil that are distinct from civil wars and interstate armed conflict. As mentioned above, instances of political upheaval that do not amount to organized armed conflict, or full-scale civil war, may also influence a state's propensity to collapse. To devise measures of generalized political unrest and instability, we use a number of indicators compiled by Banks (2012) that measure domestic political dissent and strife that do not constitute militarized conflict—either civil war or interstate conflict. These indicators include strikes, riots, antigovernment demonstrations, revolutions, government crises, coups, and guerrilla warfare. We conducted a principal-components factor analysis of these seven variables with orthogonal (varimax) rotation, which yielded two factors. The first factor was most clearly composed of the variables for strikes, riots, and demonstrations; these are mainly less intense forms of political dissent, which we refer to as political unrest. The second factor contained the indicators for more intense forms of political tumult: revolutions, coups, crises, and guerrilla warfare. We termed this factor political instability. The factor scores for these categories of political strife for each country-year constitute our variables for *Political Unrest* and *Political Instability* respectively; we expect both of these variables to be positively related to incidence of state failure.

To evaluate our hypotheses about the influence of economic factors on state collapse, we include variables for (logged) *GDP* and *Economic Openness*, the latter of which is measured as the sum of all imports and exports as a proportion of total national income. The data for these variables were acquired from the Penn World Table (Heston et al. 2002). We expect wealth, and to a lesser extent economic openness, to have a negative effect on the incidence of state failure. Wealthier states generate less dissent and may experience higher levels of stability than poorer countries because of lower levels of generalized dissatisfaction among the population. To assess effects of economic well-being, we also include a variable for economic growth on a yearly basis. Last, we control for the *Cold War*; the variable is coded 1 for each year before 1990 and zero for 1990 onward. Since we believe that the international political environment after the end of the Cold War was relatively more conducive to state collapse, we expect this variable to be negatively related to state failure. Summary statistics are provided in Table 3.1.

While we believe that our model captures most of the important systematic influences on state failure, we also recognize that there may be country-specific

TABLE 3.1: Summary Statistics

Variables	Mean	Standard deviation	Minimum	Maximum
Duration	36.56	15.97	1	66
Lagged POLITY score	0.97	7.51	−10	10
Lagged POLITY score squared	57.27	32.31	0	100
Civil War	0.15	0.36	0	1
External Armed Conflict	0.04	0.24	0	2
Lagged Political Unrest	0.05	1.08	−4.28	23.58
Lagged Political Instability	−0.03	0.96	−5.66	27.11
Lagged ln(GDP)	8.22	1.26	4.91	10.47
Lagged Economic Growth	2.35	6.98	−64.56	122.23
Lagged Economic openness	64.08	45.35	2.32	443.18
Cold War	0.53	0.50	0	1

$NT = 6573$

differences among our cases that are not included in the model specified above. We therefore need to take into account country-specific factors, other than the determinants of state failure included in the model that might influence a state's likelihood of collapse. To assess the effect of the influences discussed above on the likelihood of state failure during the period 1946 to 2009,[7] as well as to account for influences not captured by the covariates, we employ a Cox model with "frailties." "Frailty models . . . allow for individual heterogeneity in the form of a subject-specific term that captures that particular observation's unobserved propensity toward the event of interest" (Box-Steffensmeier et al. 2003). The model is expressed as:

$$h_i(t) = h_0(t)\alpha_i \exp(X_{it}\beta)$$

Similar to a "random effects" model, a Cox model with frailties allows for country-specific effects. As a result, states with similar coefficient estimates for certain covariates may be more or less vulnerable to failure given this "unobserved frailty." Using this estimation technique allows us not only to assess the hypothesized influences on state failure but also to estimate the "frailty" of states after controlling for their performance on the covariates. This model, therefore, provides an estimate of which states are more prone to failing because of some underlying propensity that is not captured by the coefficient estimates for the independent variables.

The results for the Cox model with frailties are presented in Table 3.2; in addition to the coefficient estimates, we also report hazard ratios for easier interpre-

TABLE 3.2: A Cox Model of State Failure (1952–2009)

Variables	Coefficient estimates	Hazard ratios
Lagged POLITY score	0.12 (0.08)	1.13
Lagged POLITY score squared	−0.01 (0.01)	0.98
Civil War	3.07** (0.77)	21.58
External Armed Conflict	1.48* (0.85)	4.41
Lagged Unrest	0.45* (0.22)	1.57
Lagged Instability	0.41* (0.20)	1.51
Lagged ln(GDP)	−1.79** (0.64)	0.17
Lagged Economic Growth	−0.03 (0.04)	0.97
Lagged Economic Openness	−0.02 (0.02)	0.98
Cold War	1.02 (0.84)	2.78
Theta	17.30 (10.74)	—
NT	6573	6573

Note: Cell entries are coefficient estimates; numbers in parentheses are robust standard errors, clustered by nation. One asterisk indicates $p < .05$, two indicate $p < .01$ (one-tailed).

tation of the effect of the covariates on the risk of state failure. The coefficients for the democracy variables indicate a curvilinear relationship between levels of democracy and the hazard for state failure, but this relationship is weak. In previous analyses that focused on the period from 1946 to 2000, the evidence for such a curvilinear relationship was much stronger, causing us to speculate whether systemic changes occurred in the decade of 2000 to 2009 that made democratic transitions less disruptive. One dynamic that comes to mind is the often-effective intervention by third parties and international agencies in situations of rapid democratization that may very well reduce the likelihood of those states failing or collapsing as their regimes transition (as will be discussed in Chapter Five). We should note that our model does not take into account the direction of regime transition. More states in the system, however, are moving toward democracy than autocracy, and it would be reasonable to expect that regime transition in that direction is less likely to lead to collapse than the alternative.

Nonetheless, regime change—especially rapid transitions—should not be minimized as a correlate of state failure, since we know it to have been an important influence until 2000. In previous work, one of the authors has discussed why we should be interested in such transitional or "mid-range" states (Starr 1991, 1997). By looking at "partially free" (PF) states in the Freedom House dataset (as opposed to "Free" or "Non-Free" states), for example, we can see how this condition can be conceptualized as a stopover, or way station, to or from more fully democratic or authoritarian governmental systems. In this sense countries coded as PF are of particular interest because they are "ready" to go one way or the other. In the study of the diffusion of democracy, there were only a handful of cases in the Freedom House dataset, which was used to generate governmental transitions from 1973 to 1993, in which countries moved directly from Free to Non-Free or from Non-Free to Free. Almost all of the transitions were movements into or away from the PF condition.

The most potent positive influence on the hazard of state failure is the incidence of civil war. Involvement in a civil war increases the risk of a state failing by 21.58 times (more than 2,000 percent). This finding is intuitive, since civil wars are the single most destabilizing event for a state. International conflict also increases the risk of state collapse, albeit to a much smaller extent than civil wars. Involvement in each additional external conflict in a year increases the risk that a state would collapse by 3.4 times (more than 300 percent). Similarly, both our variables for domestic political strife—political unrest and instability—reveal a positive effect on the hazard of state collapse; unrest increases that hazard by about 57 percent and instability by about 50 percent.

Although there is no statistically significant influence of economic openness and growth on state failure, national income exercises a significant and negative influence. As we expected, states with higher levels of wealth are more likely to experience internal stability and are less likely to experience a failure. Moreover, it is important to note that economic growth does not have a direct ameliorating effect on the likelihood of state collapse; it is necessary for states to achieve a certain (higher) level of economic well-being.

Our expectations regarding the negative effect of the Cold War on incidence of state failure were borne out in the earlier analysis, which did not include the most recent decade, but that effect does not seem to hold for the longer time period. This finding seems to fit Van de Walle's warning against "exaggerating the impact of the Cold War on African politics" (2004, 109). The finding also reflects that while changes in the global political environment in the immediate aftermath of the Cold War made states more prone to failing, that effect has stabilized (and diminished) over time, in part because other sources of aid replaced aid provided by the United States and the USSR. Earlier we argued that state failure was not found before World War II in part because of possible coercive absorption by nearby powers taking advantage of a power vacuum in the failed state. We had presented the plausible argument that during the Cold War the two superpowers would prop up potential failed states—and that this ended with the end of the Cold War. However, the end of the Cold War also promoted major power cooperation within the United Nations, which worked with member states and regional organizations to deal with failing states. This can be seen below in Chapter Five in analyzing the causes of second failures (see also Van de Walle 2004, 109–11).

Our analysis, therefore, provides several important insights into the causes of state failure as reflected by a complete collapse of central authority in a state. First, we find that states that are either "mixed" or transitioning from one form of regime to another—that is, with scores in the middle of the POLITY scale—may be more prone to failure than either extremely autocratic or highly democratic countries, but that effect has become less salient over time. Next, we find that instances of domestic political disturbances, ranging from unrest to civil war, are associated with state failure, with civil wars being by far the most significant determinant of state collapse. Generally, wealthier states are better positioned to avoid failure. Therefore, poorer states without well-established political institutions and domestic strife call for special attention, particularly in the post–Cold War era.

Our findings thus reinforce the results of those studies on which our hypotheses have been based. However, in the present study we have focused on "failed" states—with state failure as an endpoint or condition. Most of these other studies start with a stronger policy focus, and are concerned with a process in which at-risk, fragile, or failing states find themselves. For such policy-oriented analysts, the problem is to understand the process in order to know how to intervene effectively to slow, halt, or reverse it. As noted above, a number of such studies have research design problems with the circularity of independent and dependent variables. By avoiding such problems, we are more confident in the validity of our results. Our dependent variable also permits the use of hazard analyses, and the presentation of results that clearly show how a factor increases or decreases the hazard of failure (collapse). At the same time we next address the concern with identifying those states that are "frail" or "at risk," through the use of frailty analysis.

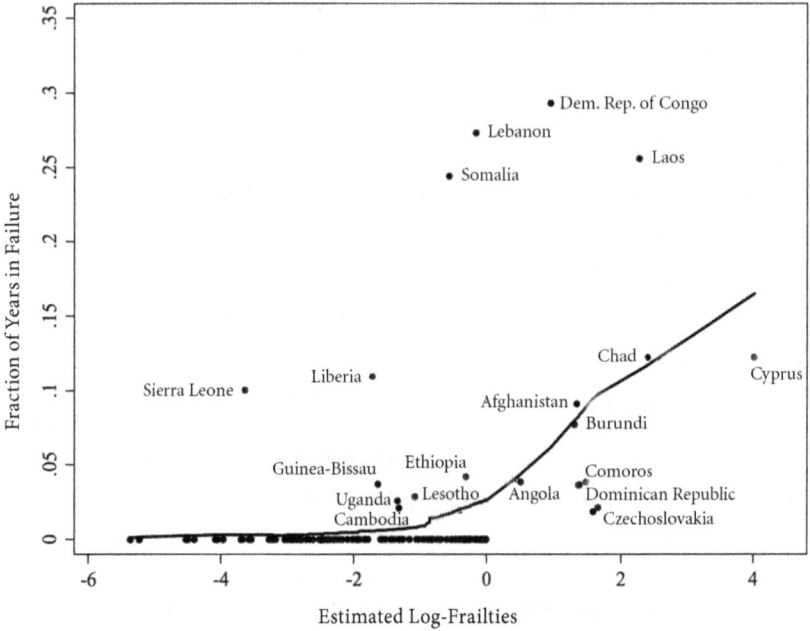

FIG. 3.1: Lowess Plot of State Failure Incidence, by Estimated Frailty

Our model also provides empirical estimates of the country-specific frailty values, which reflect a state's underlying propensity for failure after controlling for the influence of the covariates. Figure 3.1 plots the estimated log-frailties for each country against the fraction of years in our data during which that state was considered "failed." These estimated unit effects provide insight into the latent effect of state frailty, and thus serve as indicators of the propensity of states to fail conditional on the covariates. These estimates suggest, for example, that a state with a log-frailty value of approximately 1.5 (such as Comoros) is 4.4 times more likely to collapse than a state with a log-frailty value of zero. Note that some states in the data have relatively low frailty values—including Sierra Leone and Liberia—yet have failed during about 10 percent of the years under study. Such low frailty values indicate that these states actually failed less than one would have expected, given their values on the covariates. Other states with higher estimated frailties display high incidences of states failure; for instance, the Democratic Republic of Congo has a frailty estimate of approximately 4.5 and experienced a failure during 29 percent of the years under consideration (and is one of the double-failure states examined in Chapter Five). These frailty estimates thus contribute to the identification of vulnerable states by enabling us to capture a dimension of the likelihood of failure that goes beyond the performance of cases on the covariates; hence two states with identical coefficient estimates for the independent variables may display very different frailty levels, and thus have varying degrees of susceptibility to failure.

Employing a dependent variable that avoids issues of endogeneity and identification of the "frailty" of states enables us to examine state fragility and failure in a more insightful and thorough manner than afforded by previous conceptualizations of state failure. Our model identifies key determinants of state failure and analyzes their influence, as well as providing estimates of a latent dimension of states' likelihood to collapse through country-specific estimated frailties.

CONCLUSION

The results of our analysis confirm some theoretical expectations, but also run contrary to a number of other expectations in the growing literature on state failure. The effect of democracy is not linear—the hazards of state failure are the least at the highest and lowest levels of democracy. While intuition might suggest that the impact of democracy is linear—that as democracy "increases," the hazard of failure decreases—this is not the case. In line with a number of other analyses, we find that states are most vulnerable during some transitional phase, or in a condition that lacks either normative democratic constraints or nondemocratic coercive constraints. Moreover, it is somewhat surprising that the effects of external armed conflict in making states more prone to failure are not much greater than the combined effect of strikes, riots, and demonstrations. This implies that involvement in a war—if it is not fought entirely on one's own territory among domestic factions—does not tremendously increase the risk that a state will collapse.[8] Our analyses are also distinct in that they identify the effects of an underlying "frailty" on the propensity of states to collapse. One important implication of the frailty estimates is that there are clearly state-specific factors at work (as should be expected), and that any subsequent research agenda should include case studies to complement the empirical analyses.

We have thus identified a set of key explanatory factors, rather than traits or features that are used for conceptual extension, telling us which observations or cases to throw into the box of "state failure." With these cases in hand we can set out an agenda of follow-on studies that include our initial concern with the diffusion and other consequences of state failure. We now have a clearer idea of what to look for if state failure does produce diffusion/contagion effects. That is, whether to look for the consequences of failure for further failure—to see if the occurrence of the features of failure increases the probability of the occurrence of the features of failure in other states in subsequent time periods.

These findings also permit us to provide and evaluate policy prescriptions for both states and international organizations in light of our results. We expect our findings to have strong implications for policy issues related to political and economic development. In Chapter Seven, our findings are used to help survey the set of policy recommendations extant in the scholarly and policy literatures, and in selecting the most promising avenues of policy choice and implementation—especially in mitigating diffusion effects and in directing our attention to those states with the greatest hazard of collapse.

Given our concern with the problems of current conceptualizations of state failure and the logical problems with the connections between the concept and how it is measured, we believe that our findings have greater validity and reliability than extant analyses. We assess the influence of key determinants on a measure of state failure that is more suitable for empirical analysis than other existing conceptualizations of state collapse. We hope that the design we have developed to analyze the causes and consequences of state failure will yield insights that will prove valuable to a number of communities—including academics, political decision-makers, practitioners, and international organizations.

4   The Duration of State Failure

INTRODUCTION

The analysis in Chapter Three established some key correlates of state failure. In this and the next chapter, we turn to the task of addressing other questions related to the processes of state failure. Specifically, this chapter examines why some states remain in a "failed" condition longer than others, while the next explores the question of why some states collapse more than once while others are able to achieve lasting recovery from failure. Here, building on the previous chapters, we assess the factors that affect the duration of periods of failure. The study of the determinants of state failure in the last chapter directed us to four factors that may precede state failure or collapse: political instability, political unrest, civil war, and interstate war. Democracy and economic openness were also confirmed as factors that are associated with the probability of state collapse. In light of similar factors that were associated with the incidence of state failure, the analysis in this chapter will examine the question of the duration of state failure. Evaluating the determinants of the length of state failure to see why some states are able to recover from failure within a relatively short time while others remain in a state of collapse for longer periods of time extends our understanding of the causes of state failure, as well as informs the analyses in subsequent chapters that deal with the recurrence and consequences of state collapse.

HOW LONG DOES STATE FAILURE LAST?

We now turn to the examination of what determines the duration of state failure. A number of states that failed during the period under consideration recuperated from collapse within a year, including Angola, Comoros, Cambodia, and Uganda. Others took three to five years to recover, including Burundi, Cyprus, Sierra Leone, and Chad. Some states, however, remained failed for more extended periods of time. For instance, the 1961 failure in Laos lasted twelve years, and Lebanon was a failed state for fifteen years, from 1975 to 1990.[1] We expect the same factors that influence the onset of a state failure (see Chapter Three) to be associated with its duration, and we use a Cox proportional hazards model to empirically analyze the impact of these factors. We include all state failures from 1960 to 2010 in our analysis. For this time period, the model includes twenty-seven state failures (for a total of one hundred years of state failure), three of which get censored because these states had not recovered from collapse by the year in which our data set ends. Below we describe our measure of state failure and outline our expectations for the key sociopolitical influences on the length of time that state failures last, followed by the results of the empirical model.

Recall that we conceptualize state failure as a complete collapse of the central authority of a sovereign state. As in the previous chapter, we employ the −77 code in the POLITY IV data (Marshall and Jaggers 2011) as our measure of state failure. As discussed earlier, this conceptualization of state failure avoids conflation of indicators and determinants, or the dependent and independent variables, and thus better deals with problems of circularity (or endogeneity) than other measures used in studies of state failure.[2] We consider, therefore, only the −77 countries to be failed; these are states without any (institutions serving the functions of a) central government.

Most studies of state failure emphasize the importance of democracy for state stability, which leads to the expectations that the level of democracy a state supported before its collapse would be negatively associated with the length of time it remains failed. States with higher levels of democracy generally have more stable and well-established domestic political institutions, and thus governments in these states are more likely to re-emerge within a short period of time. Thus a combination of institutional memory and democratic norms may be expected to decrease the duration of failure in such states. We, however, do not expect there to be a strong positive relationship between democracy and the "hazard" of state failure termination.

Our expectation regarding the relationship between the duration of state failure and regime type is influenced by our conceptualization of state failure. We consider a state to be failed only if its central authority and governing institutions have completely collapsed. It is reasonable to argue that stable democratic institutions would be less likely to experience such utter breakdown. But once this collapse has occurred, democracy or autocracy plays no role in recovery from state failure. At that point, a previously democratic state has no advantage over other types of regimes. To assess this effect, we include a variable for regime type, measured by the *Pre-Failure POLITY score* in a state. POLITY IV scores (Marshall and Jaggers 2011) range from −10 to 10, with −10 representing the lowest level of democracy and 10 the highest. The POLITY scores of states in our sample (in the year before they collapsed) range from −8 to 8. We use the POLITY score in the last year before failure for the entire period that a state remains collapsed (that is, the years that are coded −77 in the POLITY data set). We expect the value of this "pre-failure" regime type to have little or no impact on the length of time it takes a state to recover from a collapse, inasmuch as during the years that it is a failed state, it has no government, and the level of democracy it previously supported does not exist during that time.

We include two independent variables to assess the impact of armed conflict on failure duration. We measure the presence of *Civil War* in a country-year through a dichotomous variable: 1 if there is a civil war, zero otherwise. We also include a binary variable for the presence of *External Armed Conflict*. The data for civil and international wars were acquired from the PRIO/Uppsala dataset on armed conflict (Strand et al. 2004; Gleditsch et al. 2002). We expect both types of armed conflict to have a positive effect on the duration of state failure because of violent conflict's destabilizing effect on domestic governance and the hindrance conflict may pose to re-establishing national institutions in a failed state. The civil war variable is lagged one year to account for the effect of time; external armed conflict is not lagged, because of lack of variation.

We also assess the effect of domestic political turmoil (short of civil war) on the duration of state failure; we include two variables that measure phenomena of internal turmoil that are distinct from civil wars and interstate armed conflict. For these measures of generalized political unrest and instability, we use a number of indicators compiled by Banks (2012) that measure domestic political dissent and strife. These indicators include strikes, riots, antigovernment demonstrations, revolutions, government crises, coups, and guerrilla warfare. We arrived at two factors through a principal-components factor analysis of these seven variables with orthogonal (varimax) rotation. The first factor was most clearly composed of the variables for strikes, riots, and demonstrations; these are mainly less intense forms of political dissent, which we refer to as political unrest. The second factor contained the indicators for more intense

TABLE 4.1: Summary Statistics

Variables	Mean	Standard deviation	Minimum	Maximum
Duration	5.34	4.83	1	20
Pre-Failure POLITY score	−1.27	6.06	−8	8
Lagged Civil War	0.56	0.50	0	1
External Armed Conflict	0.02	0.14	0	1
Lagged Unrest	0.04	0.84	−0.76	4.77
Lagged Instability	1.05	1.13	−0.48	5.74
Lagged ln(GDP)	7.04	1.33	4.76	10.17
Lagged ln(Economic Openness)	3.43	1.51	0.03	5.90
Lagged Economic Growth	−4.08	20.51	−65.31	85.75
Lagged ln(Population)	8.64	1.18	6.11	10.90
Second Failure	1.16	0.37	0	2
Year	1990.39	12.58	1961	2010

$NT = 100$

forms of political upheaval: revolutions, coups, crises, and guerrilla warfare. We refer to this factor as political instability. The factor scores for these categories are indicated by our variables for *Political Unrest* and *Political Instability* respectively; these variables are lagged one year and we expect these variables to be positively related to state failure duration, which is to say negatively related to failure termination.

We also include variables for (logged) *GDP* (per capita in U.S.$/1000), *GDP Growth*, (logged) *Economic Openness* (the sum of all imports and exports as a proportion of total national income), and (logged) *Population*. The data for these variables were acquired from the Penn World Table (Heston et al. 2011). We expect wealth (both GDP and economic growth) as well as economic openness to have a negative effect on the duration of state failure; this is based on the expectation that wealthier states will be less devastated by a collapse and have greater resources for recovery (see, for example, Hoeffler 2010; Chauvet et al. 2006; Marshall and Cole 2009; Chauvet and Collier 2008). We include a dummy variable for *Second Failure* to assess whether recurrent failures last longer than first failures. And we control for *Year*. Summary statistics are provided in Table 4.1.

The results for the Cox model are presented in Table 4.2. Figure 4.1 plots the Kaplan-Meier estimate of the survival function for state failure duration, along with its 95 percent confidence interval. The survival function can be thought of as the probability that a given state failure lasts a particular length of time. So, for example, Figure 4.1 suggests that we would estimate the probability of a state failure lasting five years to be 0.74 (with a 95 percent confidence interval of [0.65, 0.82]). The estimate in Figure 4.1 suggests that, in general, the length

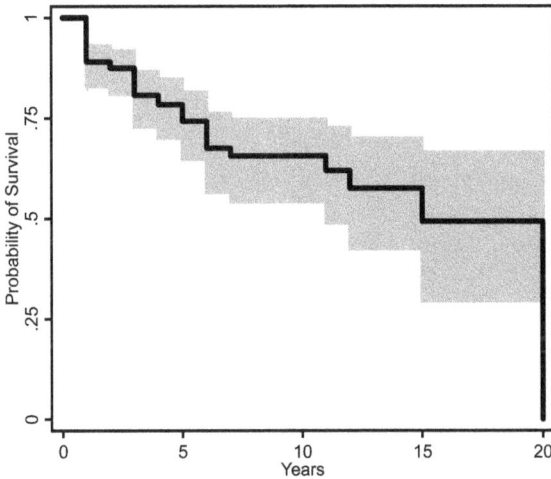

FIG. 4.1: Estimated Probabilities of State Failure Cessation

of state failures is a "long-tailed" phenomenon. A significant number of failure episodes are of relatively short duration; the probability of a state failure ending declines rapidly during its first five years. Failure episodes that survive this initial period, however, are especially long lived; the expected survival probability declines only slightly (from 0.67 to 0.57) between years six and fourteen of the failure.

Among the conflict and political violence variables, instability is the only influence that reveals a significant effect on state failure duration. The hazard ratio indicates that a one-unit (that is, one standard deviation) increase in instability is associated with a 45 percent decrease in the hazard of state failure's end. Put differently, in any given year failed states with higher levels of instability can expect their episode of state failure to be about 45 percent less likely to come to an end than similar states with lower levels of instability. Interestingly, among the economic variables, only the estimated effect of economic openness supports our expectations regarding the duration of state failures. The hazard ratio for GDP indicates that a one-unit change in (logged, lagged) GDP—that is, a doubling of nominal GDP—is associated with a reduction in the hazard of about 69 percent. In real terms, this means that failed states with a given level of GDP can be expected to have their episode of state failure last about three times longer than one with a per capita GDP half as large. In combination with the results in Chapter Three, this suggests that countries with higher levels of eco-

TABLE 4.2: A Cox Model of State Failure (1960–2010)

Variables	Coefficient estimates	Hazard ratios
Pre-Failure POLITY score	0.09	1.09
	(0.110)	
Lagged Civil War	0.15	1.16
	(0.482)	
External Armed Conflict	1.08	2.92
	(0.853)	
Lagged Unrest	0.45	1.57
	(0.549)	
Lagged Instability	−0.60*	0.55
	(0.352)	
Lagged ln(GDP)	−1.18	0.31
	(0.466)	
Lagged ln(Economic Openness)	1.07**	2.92
	(0.403)	
Lagged Economic Growth	0.01	1.01
	(0.014)	
Lagged ln(Population)	0.08	1.08
	(0.348)	
Second Failure	−3.77*	0.42
	(1.572)	
Year	−0.04*	0.02
	(0.021)	
NT	100	100

Note: Cell entries are coefficient estimates; numbers in parentheses are robust standard errors, clustered by nation. One asterisk indicates $p < .05$, two indicate $p < .01$ (one-tailed).

nomic wealth and development—while less likely to experience a state failure in the first place—are also more seriously impacted by such failures when they occur, and take longer to recover from such episodes than their less developed counterparts. Substantively, openness acts as a strong counter to these findings for GDP: a one-unit (that is, doubling) of openness increases the hazard of state failure's end by nearly threefold. This is a near-symmetrical effect to that of GDP, suggesting that while economically developed states exhibit difficulty in recovering from state failures, more open economies have the opposite effect. This suggests that states that are more involved in the international economy through trade are better able to recover from collapse, regardless of levels of

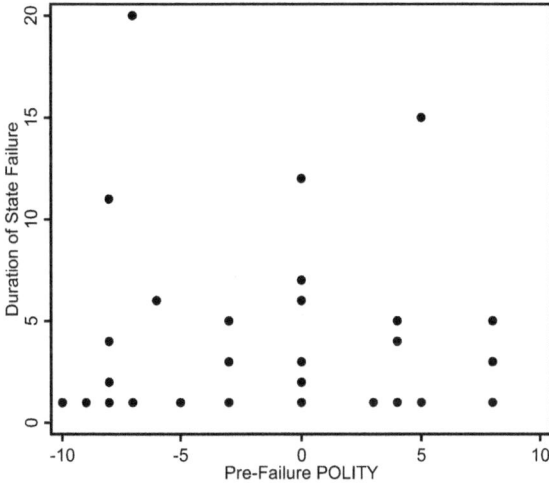

FIG. 4.2: Democracy and the Duration of State Failure

economic growth or the overall size of the economy (since GDP per capita does not have a significant effect on duration).

As we expected, the level of democracy before a state fails does not have an impact on how quickly it is able to reinstate a central government. This finding is understandable if we consider the nature of our measure of state failure. Once a state has reached the point where it no longer has a central authority and its political system has completely collapsed, the "memory" of democracy will not be enough for re-creation of a government. This confirms that what we are measuring is indeed a thorough demise of a state's leadership and political institutions. Figure 4.2 shows the (lack of) relationship between democracy and the duration of state failure. Although this finding is rather grim, it is perhaps more encouraging that armed conflict (both domestic and international) as well as political unrest and instability are also not significantly related to state failure duration. Recurrence of failure does, however, have a significant effect on the duration of collapse, which is to say that second failures are more likely than initial failures to last a long time.

We also note substantial all-else-equal differences in the durations of first and subsequent failure episodes. Specifically, second and subsequent failures have significantly lower hazards than "first" failures; substantively, this implies that second failures are expected to last much longer than first-time failure events. This is unsurprising, and in fact squares with a number of our other empirical findings. Finally, all else equal, more recent state failures have tended to be of longer duration. This is true even after adjusting for censoring (as a result of cases in which state failure was ongoing as of 2010). The magnitude of this effect is relatively small; the hazard ratio indicates that each passing year decreases the conditional probability of a state failure episode ending by about 4 percent.

Unfortunately, these results do not leave us with too many clear insights for policy prescriptions to expedite the recovery of failed states. The most important implication of this analysis comes from the negative effect of economic openness on failure duration, and reflects the desirability of international engagement by states (see de Soysa and Fjelde 2010 for similar positive effects on civil war onsets). Although the engagement in the international system measured by the openness variable captures only trade, we believe that other forms of positive interactions at the regional and global levels would also aid in recovery from state failure. In light of this finding, one possible influence on failure duration that is not included in this quantitative model is intervention by international institutions; such a systematic examination offers a useful future direction for research on state failure termination (but is, indeed, addressed in regard to the case studies of recurrence in the following chapter).

To explore the dynamics of state failure further, we consider the association between two characteristics of failure events and a range of state-level outcomes. Our first such variable, *Failure Duration*, is operationalized as the number of years that the failure in question lasted. The second, *Second Failure*, is a dichotomous indicator, coded 1 if a given failure event was the second such event for that country in our data, and zero otherwise (that is, for "first" failures). In both instances, we examine the bivariate association between these two aspects of state failure and our state characteristics variables.[3] We expect that, in general, both longer-lasting and second failures will be associated with more negative outcomes (that is, lower levels of democracy, wealth, growth, and openness, and higher levels of unrest and instability). Table 4.3 presents the results of our analyses of the associations between our two aspects of state failure and six key state-level outcomes.

In each instance, the values of the "dependent" variables were measured in the first year after the end of the failure event in question. Column I presents bivariate (Spearman) correlations between the duration of each failure event and our outcome variables, while column II presents t-tests for the difference of means in the outcome variables between first (=0) and second (=1) failures.

TABLE 4.3: Bivariate Associations between State Failure and
Relevant Outcome

Variables	Failure duration (I)	Second failure (II)
POLITY score	0.11	2.98
	(0.67)	(0.13)
Unrest	0.10	−2.04
	(0.69)	(0.01)
Instability	−0.15	0.68
	(0.55)	(0.78)
ln(GDP)	−0.26	1.33
	(0.30)	(0.03)
ln(Economic Openness)	0.08	−0.39
	(0.74)	(0.78)
Economic Growth	0.55	0.96
	(0.02)	(0.45)

Note: (I) are Spearman correlations; (II) are t-tests; *p*-values in parentheses. $NT=20$

On balance, there are few important associations between the duration of a state failure and other important national-level factors. Lengthy state failures are slightly associated with lower levels of political instability and GDP post failure, though the statistical significance of both relationships is weak. The only association to approach conventional levels of statistical importance is the positive association between failure duration and GDP growth, suggesting that countries that experience longer episodes of failure exhibit higher levels of economic growth post failure than those whose failure episodes are shorter. On average, states recovering from second failure events exhibit higher levels of political and social unrest and lower levels of GDP than first-failure states. The difference in unrest is particularly stark, reflecting an average difference of nearly two standard deviations on the unrest scale. At the same time, we observe no important differences in levels of democracy, political instability, openness, or GDP growth between first- and subsequent-failure states.

CONCLUSION

When studying the causes of state failure, the literature identifies a group of variables and factors that we have used as our basis for looking at the causes of state failure (deriving from our more highly specified concept of state collapse) and the diffusion of state failure. These variables/factors are important in understanding state failure in a feedback loop that is needed to clarify the concept. However, we now know, and have shown, that these are not the same variables/factors involved in the study of the recovery from state failure and the duration of state failure.

In the previous chapters we raised a number of issues involved in the conceptualization and operationalization of state failure, and particularly the ramifications for research design when scholars use different conceptualizations to deal with different concerns (for example, basic versus applied research) and different questions. The present chapter exemplifies these points. It provides evidence that different questions—different aspects of some complex concept or phenomenon—lead to different answers with different implications. Thus, for recovery and duration of state collapse, we find that a set of factors that relate to openness/interaction with the external system/region are central (for instance, trade, IGO membership, and so forth). These factors are *not* the same as the set of factors that appear so important to the causes of state failure (in terms of our focus on state collapse as operationalized by a –77 status). While we will see how the *causal* factors investigated in Chapter Three play out in the *diffusion* of the consequences of state failure in Chapter Six, we also find these openness/interaction factors relating to international engagement to be equally important in explaining the *recurrence* of state failure, which is the focus of the next chapter. Finally, the answers to questions about *all* of the different faces of state failure, and the processes involved, are relevant to our consideration of the policy alternatives about how to deal with state failure discussed in Chapter Seven.

5   Recurrent Collapse and Its Causes

INTRODUCTION

We are interested in state failure, in large part, because of the concern by policy-makers and academics alike with the *effects* and *impact* of state failure. As noted in the introductory chapter, investigating such impacts was a primary motivation for our study. In that sense, this chapter—as well as the one to follow—is about studying the *consequences* of state failure. Does a state failure lead to more state failure? We turn in this chapter to the question of why some states that fail achieve a lasting recovery, while others experience a recurrence of failure. We focus on four specific cases of recurrent state failure. Afghanistan experienced its first state collapse in 1978, recovered the next year, and collapsed again in 1992. The Democratic Republic of the Congo (DRC) was a failed state from 1960 to 1963, and it failed again in 1992. Ethiopia first failed for one year in 1974, and again in 1991. The fourth repeated failure occurred in the Ivory Coast, where the first (year-long) collapse happened in 2006 and the second in 2010.

In order to assess the factors that caused these states to fail twice, we undertake a series of four comparative case studies, comparing each of these four states to similar states that experience only a single failure during this period. This comparison is designed to offer insights into the specific factors that might lead to recurrent failure in some states. We adopt a similar-systems approach, comparing states that are most similar with each other on a number of relevant dimensions. The motivation behind this choice of research design is that if similar states were able to avoid recurrent collapse, why did these four states fall prey to a second collapse?

In order to decide on the factors for comparison, we draw upon the previous chapters, and use the variables employed as covariates in the empirical models in those analyses (and thus have both a theoretical and empirical basis for inclusion).[1] For the selection of matching cases, we adopt a variant of propensity score matching based on Mahalanobis distance (Morgan and Winship 2007). In addition to maximizing the degree of similarity between cases so matched, an advantage of this approach is that it does so while accounting for the intrinsic covariation among the variables on which the matching takes place. The result of our matching procedure yields four states among the failed states in our data that are most similar to the four states that experience a second, or recurrent, failure. Each of the states with repeated collapse is matched with the state that is most similar to it in light of the relevant influences. This matching exercise produced the following set of comparative cases:[2]

Double-Failure States	Matched Case
Afghanistan (1978, 1992)	Guinea-Bissau (1998)
Ethiopia (1974, 1991)	Uganda (1985)
Democratic Republic of Congo (1962, 1992)	Cambodia (1975)
Ivory Coast (2006, 2010)	Solomon Islands (2002)

Based on factors raised in the state failure literature, and employed in our earlier analyses, thirteen variables were used for determining the single-failure matched cases (matched on the first year of the first failure of each of our states). These tapped the duration of the initial failure, whether there were contiguous state failures, and the number of state failures in the global system.[3] Economic variables included GDP, growth in GDP, and economic openness. Both the POLITY governmental score and the POLITY score squared were used. The set of conflict variables included unrest, instability, a conflict count, and conflict type. Except for the duration of the initial failure, all of the variables were lagged.

Keeping in mind that the four pairs of cases have already been matched on a number of factors, what does the context and history of collapse in each of the countries tell us that could help to distinguish the cases with two different outcomes (single-collapse states versus repeat-collapse states)? We will first turn to another broad set of overview variables that will expand upon and add to those factors used to identify our matched pairs.

BASIC DIMENSIONS FOR COMPARISON: SYSTEMIC LINKAGES

In the original matching exercise, we looked at one aspect of geopolitical factors—contiguous failures, as well as failures in the system as a whole. These factors raise questions about the effects of borders, and more general questions about a variety of connections that states have to the international system.

These will be looked at separately from other internal factors, such as government performance, additional economic factors, components of legitimacy, and the like. Country-specific chronologies of events, internal conflict, external interventions (which include regional and UN missions of various kinds), and peace treaties will be detailed more fully in the following section.

Given the important finding about economic openness and international engagement in the last chapter, we need also to ask what sorts of ties do states, and failed states in particular, have with other states and nonstate actors in the international system? Could these ties play a role in protecting a state that has failed once from a second collapse? It has been long known that proximity and higher levels of interaction can promote both higher levels of conflict as well as higher levels of cooperation. Can systematic effects be found that distinguish single- and double-failure states?

Starr (2005 and 2009) has looked at proximity and contiguous borders, revealing the conditions under which they might promote conflict (and instability) or cooperation. In general, research findings have shown that a greater number of interaction opportunities—that is, a greater number of contiguous borders—increases the probability of interstate conflict. Indeed, large numbers of studies control for contiguity just because of this effect. We may begin then with a simple comparison of the number of contiguous borders for our matched cases as seen in Table 5.1. The table indicates that in three of the four matched cases, the double-failures had more bordering/contiguous states, with the single-failure Solomon Islands having no contiguous borders. Thus, as one sort of linkage to other international actors involves the opportunities for conflict, and especially the internationalization of internal conflict, having large numbers of contiguous neighbors appears to be a feature of the double-failure group.

In addition, in Table 5.1 we have included two additional measures, taking into account the "nature" of contiguous borders developed by Starr (for example, 2002). Going beyond a dichotomous "on/off" view of borders, Starr used GIS methodology to develop a measure for "ease of interaction" for any segment of a border, or the border as a whole. That is, we can go beyond simply saying there was or was not a contiguous border, and investigate to what extent the border was permeable—or easy to cross by military capabilities or for trade. Because interaction opportunities, particularly ease of interaction, were also found to be associated with higher levels of transactions, and thus could produce positive interdependence or integration effects, Starr and Thomas (2005)

TABLE 5.1: The Number and Nature of Contiguous Borders for the Matched Cases

Cases	#of borders	avg. ease	avg. salience	Cases	#of borders	avg. ease	avg. salience
Afghanistan	6	2.35	1.042	DRC/Congo	9	2.656	1.033
Guinea-Bissau	**2**	**3.0**	**1.00**	**Cambodia**	**3**	**2.79**	**1.018**
Ethiopia	5	2.68	1.001	Ivory Coast	5	2.955	1.001
Uganda	**5**	**2.556**	**1.008**	**Solomon Islands**	**0**	**—**	**—**

investigated the relationship between ease of interaction and conflict. Ease of interaction was found to have an inverted-U-shaped effect on the levels of conflict—with low conflict when ease of interaction was either very low or very high (Starr and Thomas 2005).

The average ease of interaction for the four double-failures was 2.66, and for the three matched cases with borders, 2.80. Both groups were higher than the world mean score for ease of interaction of 2.597 (but lower than the world median of 2.8). In two cases the single-failure measure of ease was higher, and in two cases it was lower. This brief overview would imply that for our analyses, the older and simpler view holds: that having more neighbors creates the opportunity for more problems—especially given the geopolitical neighborhoods within which the double-failures reside.[4] Having no patterns for the scores on ease of interaction does not allow us to posit possible positive effects of ease of movement across borders. Similarly, a measure for "salience," or the importance of a border, was developed. However, as seen in Table 5.1, the salience scores are similarly indeterminate. This is a first indication that the more in-depth analysis of conflict will be important.

As suggested in Chapter Four, would a country's broad set of ties with the international community help buffer it against a second failure? This can be approached by investigating overall membership in international organizations, and then specifically looking at ties that are created through economic organizations. Two data sets are used to address overall IGO membership. The first is the IGO membership data set created by the Correlates of War Project (COW). The other data set is the Membership in Conventional Intergovernmental Organizations (Marshall et al. 1999). The measure used is CIOTOT, for total number of organizations.[5]

As Table 5.2 indicates, for two of our matched cases—Afghanistan/Guinea Bissau and Ethiopia/Uganda—there is a clear difference in the level of interac-

TABLE 5.2: Connections with the International System: IGO Memberships

Cases	COW total	CIOTOT	Cases	COW total	CIOTOT
Afghanistan '78	26	16	DRC/Congo '62 ('60 data)	23	14
Guinea-Bissau '98	51	28	Cambodia '75	25	20
Ethiopia '74	23	16	Ivory Coast '06	84	ND
Uganda '85	46	43–48	Solomon Islands '02	26	ND

tion with the global system as measured by IGO membership. In both, the single-failure state shows a much higher level of membership. While only slightly higher in the case of Cambodia when compared with the DRC, the pattern continues. The one exception involves the Ivory Coast and Solomon Islands.

Thus, it appears that we need to investigate the positive effect of IGO linkages more closely. One way to begin to parse out different types of IGO membership effects would be to look at economic IGOs, specifically the number and types of economic agreements. This is another way to capture economic openness. By seeing how the economic contexts of the matched cases differ in terms of types of economic relationships, we can begin to see if such agreements could help explain how systemic involvement could buffer states from a second failure. Types of economic agreements may be scaled from the least to the highest level of economic integration. Briefly, five such levels can be identified (Shaffer 2012):

PSA: *Partial Scope Agreements* reduce barriers to trade between states but do not eliminate them for a "substantial part of the trade."

FTA: *Free Trade Agreements* eliminate barriers for a substantial part of trade such that goods generally move freely between members.

CU: *Customs Unions* include free trade *and* common external tariffs for members with respect to nonmembers.

CM: *Common Markets* include a customs union *and* reduced or eliminated restrictions on the movement of the factors of production (labor, enterprise, capital) between members.

EU: *Economic Unions* include a common market and the coordination of domestic economic practice to include fiscal and monetary policies. Two states are seen to be in an economic union if they meet the minimum requirements for a common market and share a common currency.

Taking each matched pair individually, we can see that along with greater IGO involvement in general, the single-failure states indeed had greater external economic ties and interdependencies than the double-failure countries with which they were matched.

Afghanistan/Guinea-Bissau

At the end of the first failure in 1978, Afghanistan had zero economic agreements, while after its failure Guinea-Bissau was involved in *three*. Two of these were partial scope agreements (PSA). One was the Africa, Caribbean, and Pacific–EU development cooperation arrangement (ACP-EC), based on a number of agreements, of which the Cotonou Agreement of 2000 was the most recent. At the time of the Guinea-Bissau recovery from collapse, this group of countries involved fifteen EU members. Guinea-Bissau's second agreement was with ECOWAS (the Economic Community of West African States), which linked Guinea-Bissau to eight other West African countries. The third was an economic union agreement (or highest type in the above typology—an EU) involving WAEMU (the West African Economic and Monetary Union). This connected Guinea-Bissau to seven West African countries. It is obvious that the single-failure matched case, Guinea-Bissau, had a more extensive set of formal economic linkages both regionally and with a set of highly developed economies.

Ethiopia/Uganda

In 1979 Ethiopia had but one PSA—with, at that time, the nine countries of the EU through the ACP-EC. In 1986, the single-failure Uganda also had an APC-EC with the twelve EU member countries. However, as with Guinea-Bissau, Uganda also had a regional agreement: a second PSA with the twenty-member Preferential Trade Area for Eastern and Southern Africa. While not as dramatic as the Afghanistan/Guinea-Bissau match, again the single-failure state could claim a deeper set of formal economic linkages.

Ivory Coast/Solomon Islands

A similar pattern is found in regard to the matched cases of the Ivory Coast/Solomon Islands. In 2006, the Ivory Coast engaged in one agreement: an economic union agreement with the seven states of the WAEMU, becoming the eighth member. In 2002 the Solomon Islands had two PSA agreements: one was the ACP-EC and its fifteen EU countries, while the other was SPARTECA, the South Pacific Regional Trade and Economic Cooperation Agreement with Australia and New Zealand. Importantly, while the Ivory Coast had a more integrated form of agreement—an economic union—trade data gathered for the agreement partners indicate that the Solomon Islands' agreements with EU countries, and with Australia/New Zealand, generated much higher levels of trade.

In 1962 the DRC had no economic agreements; neither did Cambodia in 1975. Thus, except for the DRC and Cambodia, both with special circumstances that might keep them cut off from such economic agreements, it appears that the single-failure matched cases had stronger economic linkages and interdependencies with other countries. This measure of economic linkage and interdependency needs to be added to the substantially higher levels of IGO involvement shown by Guinea-Bissau and Uganda (and the more modest edge that Cambodia held in comparison to the DRC) as indicators of greater systemic ties—and perhaps a greater external web of support to help prevent a second failure.

BASIC DIMENSIONS FOR COMPARISON:
LEGITIMACY AND GOVERNMENT PERFORMANCE

A useful bridge between the "Systemic Linkages" section above, and this one, would be to return to comparisons of the matched states on the autocracy-democracy scale. The spread of democracy since World War II has been well documented (for example, Starr 1991; Starr and Lindborg 2003; Huntington 1991; Ward and Gleditsch 1998). Along with the rise of democracies in the system and the decline in autocracies, Starr and Lindborg (2003), using Freedom House data, note that the number of Free (F) states in the international system pass the number of Nonfree (NF) states in 1985. Many discussions of global liberalization as well as globalization address the emergence of a new environment, dominated by liberal/democratic states, as a force leading to increased interactions among the newly democratic states, and those moving toward democracy. So while the POLITY scores of the failed states were used to help determine the matched cases, it would still be instructive to compare the set of double-failures to the single-failure matched cases on their levels of autocracy-democracy (with the mixed-governmental type of anocracies in between), and see if their levels of democracy might have had an effect on bringing other elements of the international system to their aid.

Starting with the double-failure states, we see that Afghanistan in 1978 and Ethiopia in 1974 were both solid autocracies (with POLITY scores of −7 and −9, respectively; they are both rated Nonfree [NF] by Freedom House in those years). The DRC in 1962 was not rated, as the country was emerging from colonial rule and then went directly to –77. The Ivory Coast in 2006 was rated an anocracy (with a score of 4) by POLITY; however, Freedom House rated it NF.

A clear difference emerges when contrasting the above to the single-failure matched cases. With the following POLITY scores, Guinea-Bissau (5), Uganda (3), and Cambodia (–5) were all anocracies, while their matched cases were autocracies. The double-failure Ivory Coast, as noted, was rated an anocracy. However, the Solomon Islands, its matched case, had a rating of 8 in 2002, and thus was a solid democracy.[6] Even with the two lower Freedom House ratings, it is clear that the single-failure cases were further along the governance scale in the direction of democracy than their matched double-failures. It is also important to note that if we return to the full list of countries rated –77, of the other seventeen single-failure countries that were given ratings before their failure, only *six* were rated autocracies! The rest were rated anocracies (along with two democracies, Chad and Lesotho). In Chapter Four we hypothesized that second failures would be associated with lower levels of democracy (and thus lower scores on the POLITY rankings), but no statistically significant results were found regarding duration and recovery. However, looking at our four pairs where a number of factors were closely matched, we can begin to see some of the effects of having scores in the anocracy range discriminating between double-failure and single-failure states—scores that could help explain greater willingness to have systemic ties and economic openness.

While not surprising (or perhaps even trite), these findings for the –77 countries in general, as well as for the matched cases, reflect many of the same effects scholars have found between the level of democracy and development, the occurrence of civil war, concern for the environment, use of IGOs and other conflict management techniques, and so forth (see Russett and Starr 2000 for an overview of such effects).

While the level of democracy may be used to complement other factors that represent state involvement with other actors in the global system, it might also be seen as part of a cluster of factors related to governmental performance and legitimacy. This is not the place to join the debate over exactly what makes a democracy a democracy, and what data sets best tap into those core features of the concept, or the de facto structure and behavior of democracies. One dimension of this highly complex and contested concept is, however, the existence and level of judicial independence. For example, Gibler and Randazzo (2011) discuss the various ways courts build legitimacy, and argue that courts with legitimacy can be a powerful constraining actor within governmental structures.

TABLE 5.3: Composite Measure of Judicial Independence

Cases	Judicial Independence	Cases	Judicial Independence
Afghanistan '78	.0965	DRC/Congo '62 ('60 data)	.0231
Guinea-Bissau '98	**.2304**	**Cambodia '75**	**.0734**
Ethiopia '74	.1073	Ivory Coast '06	.2587
Uganda '85	**.1223**	**Solomon Islands '02**	**.8044**

To achieve such legitimacy, courts must have judicial independence. Gibler and Randazzo (2011, 698) describe a weak version of judicial independence based on a selection effect: "Courts matter by providing constraints on the crafting of legislation." A stronger version is based on the courts maintaining the rule of law: "The stronger version of judicial independence argues that courts can play a central role in guaranteeing democratic stability." Their analysis indicates that "established independent judiciaries prevent regime changes toward authoritarianism across all types of states. Established courts are also capable of thwarting regime collapses in nondemocracies" (696).[7]

We can look at our matched cases using a composite score for judicial independence. Scores run from zero (no independence) to 1 (complete independence) and were calculated based on a Bayesian latent variable measurement model.[8] As seen in Table 5.3, although many of the scores are quite low, the lowest scores belong to double-failure cases, and each of the single-failure countries does better on judicial independence than its double-failure counterpart.

Governmental performance, a government's ability to meet the basic needs of its population, has been, as noted, one view of what makes a failed state "failed." Murph-Schwarzer (2011), notes that human security goes beyond freedom from need or freedom from fear, but must include freedom from want. Directly touching on state failure, she also notes: "As the insecurity threshold becomes unbearable, individuals are presented with two options: to either force the government to act on their behalf (often resulting in civil conflict) or to move." The growing literature on human security (for example, United Nations Development Programme 1994; Hampson et al. 2002; Mack 2005; Murph-Schwarzer 2011) has pointed to a number of indicators of "quality of life" that could operationalize human security, with many arguing that the UN Human Development Programme's Human Development Index is as good a summary measure as we have. Here, we can use HDI in only a limited way. There are major gaps in the HDI data especially for the initial failures of the double-failure group. However, using HDI scores that occur at the times of the second failures, the set of matched cases look very similar. All of them sit in the UNDP "low human development" category for the years involved. The one pair with data that approximate the first failure and the date of the matched case—Ivory Coast and the Solomon Islands—does show a bit of a gap in favor of the single-failure country: the Solomon Islands with 0.479 against Ivory Coast's 0.397 (again, both in the "low" category). A related comparison, which, again, is available only for this pair (approximating the dates for the failure cases) is life expectancy at birth. For both males and females, the Solomon Islands clearly does better than the Ivory Coast:

	Male	*Female*
Ivory Coast	51	53
Solomon Islands	63	66

This last comparison is only vaguely suggestive of better governmental performance in the single-failure cases.[9] However, Walter (2004) among others (for example, Hales and Miller 2010; Esty et al. 1998; Backer and Huth 2014) argues that *infant mortality* by itself is a good indicator of government effectiveness, "governance," and thus, logically, some aspects of legitimacy. Using the UN World Population Prospects Report (2011 report) along with information from the 2009 CIA World Factbook, we do have data for infant mortality for the correct dates for all four matched pairs. As seen in Table 5.4, three of the four single-failure cases do substantially better on this measure. The only exception is Cambodia. As will be seen in the chronology and description of the individual cases below, this is understandable given the policies of the Pol Pot regime, which killed such a large proportion of the population (including infants dying before age one per one thousand births.) Thus, along with democracy, we do have some indication that effective governance, along with greater systemic ties, has a negative effect on the recurrence of failure.

TABLE 5.4: Rates of Infant Mortality

Cases	Infant mortality rate	Cases	Infant mortality rate
Afghanistan	194.50	DRC/Congo	106.94
Guinea-Bissau	**134.10**	**Cambodia**	**180.55**
Ethiopia	140.03	Ivory Coast	77.17
Uganda	**107.64**	**Solomon Islands**	**42.88**

BASIC DIMENSIONS FOR COMPARISON: ECONOMIC FACTORS

Again, we can start with a variable that bridges government performance/ legitimacy, and an overview of economic factors. While the four sets of cases were matched on GDP and GDP growth, it would be useful for us to begin this discussion with a measure of the amount of the state's wealth *used by the government*, assuming that this measure translates into greater amounts spent on general services/public goods for society. Data for this indicator were found in the Penn World Tables as the government consumption share of PPP-converted GDP per capita ("kg," using 2005 constant prices). These data are presented in Table 5.5.

Drawing from the logic of political survival that uses the selectorate model (Bueno de Mesquita et al. 2003), some countries with certain kinds of wealth will direct that wealth to the winning coalition, and not general governmental expenditures providing for the public welfare. This may be so even in countries with greater levels of wealth.[10] In that case, using an indicator of governmental expenditure (and not simply funneling resources to a small selectorate or winning coalition) may be of some use as an indicator of one clear difference between the double-failures and their matched cases. As an indicator of governmental performance/legitimacy, as well as how a government uses its resources, we see that in all four matched pairs, the government consumption share of GDP per capita ("kg") is higher for the single-failure case, and substantially so for three of them.[11]

Another economic factor that links each country to the world, and at the same time reflects government performance, is foreign aid—or official development assistance (ODA), whether provided by a single donor state or through multilateral international organizations. Students of failed states have investigated ODA from a number of perspectives. While aid is seen as being a positive factor, more and more scholars have noted that to be effective, donors must un-

TABLE 5.5: Government Consumption as a Share of GDP per capita

Cases	kg (%)	Cases	kg (%)
Afghanistan	9.98	DRC/Congo	3.48
Guinea-Bissau	**11.09**	**Cambodia**	**6.42**
Ethiopia	5.75	Ivory Coast	6.81
Uganda	**16.26**	**Solomon Islands**	**39.97**

TABLE 5.6: Net ODA Received as a Percentage of GNI

Cases	Net ODA received (%GNI)	Cases	Net ODA received (%GNI)
Afghanistan	0.6	Ivory Coast	1.5
Guinea-Bissau	**39.9**	**Solomon Islands**	**7.7**
Ethiopia	3.4		
Uganda	**4.9**		

derstand the impact of different types of aid under various conditions. Taking a first cut at the issue of foreign aid, we will not look at absolute amounts of aid, but rather ODA received as a percentage of GNI, to see whether aid might be of enough importance to have an impact on the possibility of a second failure. These data are presented in Table 5.6 using World Bank data. Note that there are no data for the DRC/Cambodia matched pair.

In all three of the cases for which we have data, the single-failure cases receive a larger amount of foreign aid as a percentage of gross national income. The difference in the Afghanistan/Guinea-Bissau case is striking. But note also, that if one looks just one year later (2003) at the Solomon Islands, ODA as a percentage of GNI rises to 18.1 percent. Again, this measure could be lumped with economic development or the linkages/interdependencies with the global system. While not representing absolute amounts, it does provide some idea about the possible degree of impact. It also does not differentiate between categories of foreign aid, as discussed by Paul Collier and colleagues (for example, Chauvet and Collier 2008), Carment et al. (2008), or in a series of articles by Bueno de Mesquita and Smith (2007, 2009a, 2009b). We can note here, however, that along with more detailed discussions of peacekeeping and external conflict management missions (below), these data on ODA might help indicate that external international actors were trying to intervene to prevent a recurrence of failure within a country.

In studying civil war, the ability to recover from state failure (in its multiple definitions), or how foreign aid policy affects the economic development, stability, and government type of recipients, an interesting distinction has emerged regarding the nature of the aid provided. The focus of attention has been on what Bueno de Mesquita and Smith call "free goods," or what Collier, Girod (2012), and others call "windfall" income. In distinction from free goods, some aid, such as technical assistance, training programs, or specific goods targeted at specific projects or groups (such as education) are more likely to have positive effects—as demonstrated in the analyses of Chauvet and Collier (2008) regarding failed state "turnarounds." Free good aid, given in large amounts directly to recipient governments, may not only have no positive effects but may actually be harmful in making development, stability, conflict reduction, and movement toward democracy *less* likely. Indeed, Englebert and Tull (2008) lament how little there is to show for the more than $500 billion in foreign aid to Africa, with large amounts of it simply going into the pockets of "kleptocratic rulers."

Smith (2008, 780) notes that free goods are a "form of unearned resources .... They are free in the sense that they do not require the citizens to work to provide them." Collier first discussed this phenomenon as part of the "resource curse," whereby "the existence of valuable natural resources increases the payoff for subsets of the society to hold power and use it to their own advantage" (Chauvet and Collier 2008, 336). Chauvet and Collier (2008) argue that such windfall external income, whether additional rents from resource exports or foreign aid, negatively impacts reforms needed for failed states to turn around, in distinction from technical assistance or more targeted aid. This idea arises explicitly in the Bueno de Mesquita et al. (2003) model of the selectorate— where leaders in countries with small selectorates can buy them off and retain political power. In a series of papers, Bueno de Mesquita and Smith direct these arguments to the use of foreign aid as such "free goods," and their impact on the public welfare and even rebellion/revolution. They note: "Receiving aid is most likely to improve the welfare of citizens in large coalition systems [large S]. In such systems, the majority of the additional resources are allocated to public goods, and the leader can retain only limited resources for her own discretionary projects. Aid given to large S systems is likely to promote economic growth and enhance social welfare" (Bueno de Mesquita and Smith 2007, 280). This is the same observation made by Collier regarding the resource curse and aid as windfall income. Elsewhere Bueno de Mesquita and Smith (2009a, 309) conclude: "We find that aid benefits donor and recipient leaders, while harming the recipient's, but not the donor's, citizenry."[12]

Desha Girod (2012) develops a model based upon the selectorate model, looking at windfall income that, following Collier, may come from either certain natural resources and/or strategic aid. Girod argues that in countries without institutions (or with weak institutions), the leaders who are more likely to promote development after civil wars are those in countries that *lack* windfall income—that is, have "empty pockets." Without such wealth, they can only continue survival ("coup proof" themselves) by getting resources from non-

TABLE 5.7: Recurrence and Windfall Income

Afghanistan (1978):	High Windfall	Congo-DRC (measured in 1970):	High Windfall
Guinea-Bissau (1999):	**Low Windfall**	**Cambodia (1975):**	**Low Windfall**
Ethiopia (1979)	Low Windfall	Ivory Coast (measured 2001):	Low Windfall
Uganda (1986):	**Low Windfall**	**Solomons (2002):**	**NA**

strategic assistance, usually ODA from multilateral sources such as IGOs. Thus, empty pocket leaders seek, get, and implement development assistance agreements. In addition, no matter how much they steal from society, by following the conditions for accepting assistance, they are more likely to promote overall development by providing public goods, whether intended or not. Note that this argument supports the above discussion of ODA as a percentage of GNI.

What this means for the present discussion is that the single-failure matched cases would be more likely to develop, and more likely to have a more robust economic infrastructure, if they are "empty pockets" *low* windfall income countries. We can test this hypothesis with Girod's data (Table 5.7).[13] While Girod has provided data for only three of the four single-failure matched cases, a review of the Solomon Islands case indicates that it also fits: all four single-failure matched cases are categorized "Low Windfall," while half of the double-failure cases (Afghanistan and DRC) are categorized as "High Windfall." These two cases also indicate how leaders can use free goods to maintain strong autocracies, but also fail to develop the economy, and actively work to reduce the broader distribution of wealth. These results also fit with the argument that sees low legitimacy as a factor that could promote a recurrence of state failure (as well as a systemic interdependence argument.) We may posit that Low Windfall countries find themselves more fully enmeshed with IGOs, and especially IGO aid conditionality and performance, which provides greater resources to more people in weak institutionalized countries—that is, countries most likely to fail, having a tougher time to recover, and having a greater likelihood of a second failure.

BASIC DIMENSIONS FOR COMPARISON: A FIRST CUT AT CONFLICT

The more detailed individual (and matched) case studies to follow will elaborate in greater depth on the role of internal conflict and civil war in each of the cases. However, a number of broad conflict-related factors may be introduced at this point. For example, many students of conflict have focused on long-term rivalries ("enduring" rivalries) as a major source of conflict in the international system. We might develop contradictory hypotheses on how the presence of such a rivalry might promote or retard the recurrence of state failure. That is not necessary, however, as a composite list of rivalries (drawing across several major rivalry datasets; see Oh 2012) indicates that none of the double-failure countries were involved in rivalries at the time of either failure. Similarly, none of the matched cases were in enduring rivalries in the post–World War II period.

While almost all cases coded as –77 suffered some form of, or combination of, internal or external conflict prior to the coded failure, here we are concerned with the occurrence of conflict *subsequent to* an initial failure. Exactly *how* the initial conflicts developed, and how they were dealt with by the international community through regional or UN interventions or missions, will be discussed in a later section.

Let us first turn to the occurrence of conflict after the first failure for the double-failure cases. Using the UCDP/PRIO conflict data set, we see that three of the four double-failure cases (except for the Ivory Coast) had violent conflict subsequent to the first failure. Indeed, except for the Ivory Coast, the other three double-failure cases had significantly greater amounts of conflict both *before* and *after* the first failure. The DRC and Ethiopia had fighting in both of the PRIO categories for types of conflict: over control of government *and* over territory. Both cases involved continuous and significant external intervention. Afghanistan is similar in terms of external intervention, but none of its long-term conflicts was over territory. Echoing an earlier observation in Chapter Two (and Chapter Three), we also see that all three had significant elements of the –66 coding (the "interruption" period when a country is occupied by another state during war).

Turning to the matched cases, we find that only two of them had violent conflict after the initial failure: Uganda and Cambodia. Both were for control of the government, and each was coded as having both an internal conflict and an internationalized internal conflict across the years of violence. We find here some evidence that perhaps avoiding postfailure conflict might be helpful in avoiding a second failure. The Solomon Islands had no UCDP/PRIO conflicts listed for them. Guinea-Bissau (failing in 1998) had minimal conflict noted in 1998–99: internal conflict for the control of government (involving juntas but also Senegalese intervention). Both Cambodia and Uganda had significant conflict before their failures, and long stretches of conflict afterward. Cambodia dealt with Vietnam and the Khmer Rouge, Uganda with a variety of internal opposition groups. Again, we see the possibility that many of these years were actually periods of –66.

With the high levels of external intervention/participation in three of the double-failure cases—DRC, Afghanistan, and Ethiopia (with Afghanistan the clearest case)—we see the possibility of long stretches of –66, which made them more prone to a second failure. On the other hand, Cambodia may have suffered only one failure *because* of the quasi-status of –66 during the long period of Vietnamese dominance.

Looking at a set of basic dimensions for comparison as a first cut at our case studies has helped us to identify candidates that might promote or reduce the probability of the recurrence of state failure. Linkages to external systems, regional or global (such as IGO memberships and ties to economic organizations), along with elements indicating governmental legitimacy (performance in terms of human development and use of government resources, movements toward democracy, judicial independence) all seem to reduce the likelihood of a second collapse. More borders and higher levels of post-collapse conflict appear to be important factors that influence the recurrence of state failure.

We turn now to more in-depth case studies, part of which will elaborate on post-collapse conflict along with the role and effects of external interventions on stabilization or destabilization. With the use of comparative case analyses, we bring the power of multiple methods to bear, complementing the systematic quantitative analyses of earlier chapters.

MATCHED CASE STUDIES[14]

Afghanistan-Guinea Bissau

Afghanistan

Afghanistan appears to be a classic case of a failed state stemming from poverty and underdevelopment, significant ethnic conflict (seven major ethnic groups and both major Islamic sects), and autocracy—all worsened within the Cold War context of clashing ideologies and massive external intervention. The latter factor was heightened by Afghanistan's geographical location (including contiguity with the Soviet Union), and the long history of Afghan-Russian relations as part of the British-Russian imperial competition in Asia. Indeed, for most of its modern history Afghanistan has been under the influence of foreign powers. It found itself a central buffer between the British Empire and the Russian Empire, each of which provided substantial funds to the Afghani government and military. In the post–World War II era it similarly was a major part of the Cold War struggle between the United States and the USSR. A fierce struggle for control of the government between supporters of an autocratic government and Soviet-backed communist challengers, followed by massive Soviet military intervention, was clearly the main cause of Afghanistan's short collapse. This situation would reflect the Political Instability Task Force's (PITF) "complex" conflict (see Hales and Miller 2010, 25). The collapse in 1978 was followed by firm autocratic governmental control, with Soviet backing, as the internal conflict led by the Mujahideen developed.

The historical context for Afghanistan's collapse is succinctly presented in the 2010 POLITY IV Country Report:

> Up until the 1973 coup, Afghanistan was governed under a monarchical system that had its foundation in the Mohammadzai clan of the Durrani Pashtun Tribal Confederation. Afghanistan's last king, Mohammad Zahir Shah, reigned from 1933 to 1973 and oversaw a brief experiment with political liberalization in the mid-1960s. However, deep ethnic, class and ideological divisions within Afghanistan triggered the 1973 coup by former Prime Minister Sardar Mohammad Daoud and brought an abrupt end to the process of democratization in this country. The demise of the monarchy in 1973 ushered in an era of chronic political instability[15] that would last for much of the next three decades and would result in the invasion of Soviet troops, the formation of an Islamic theocracy and, ultimately, the economic and political collapse of Afghani society.

Muhammad Daoud Khan gained control of the government in 1973 in a bloodless coup. Among other policies attempting social and economic reform, he moved to repress the growing Islamic movement. In 1978, the People's Democratic Party of Afghanistan (PDPA) led the Khaql uprising against Daoud. Despite the ideological overlay, within the Khaql there were ethnic divisions between the Ghilzai tribe and the Durrani (the tribe of the monarchy and the Daoud regime). In April 1978, the Afghan Army, which had been sympathetic to the cause, overthrew and executed Daoud along with members of his family. Nur Muhammad insurgent troops, armed with Soviet MiGs and SU-7s assisted the PDPA in the government takeover.

The PDPA, taking advantage of both Soviet support and widespread discontent, moved to implement a socialist agenda, which included state atheism, land reform, and torturing of elites. Note that military cooperation between the USSR and Afghanistan had been established since 1956, and that further agreements were the basis for the presence of Soviet military advisers in the 1970s, creating ties with the Afghani military. In December 1978 a new treaty permitted the PDPA to ask the Soviet Union for military support. This became crucial as the PDPA policies led to open rebellion in many parts of Afghanistan, led by mullahs and other traditional elites. In the midst of PDPA factional conflict and several changes in leadership, the Afghan government requested Soviet military aid based on the December 1978 treaty. On December 24, 1979, the first elements of the Soviet 40th Army were deployed. The period from December 1979 to February 1980 is considered the period of Soviet occupation.

Regarding the post-failure period, there were no peace agreements after 1978, simply a Soviet occupation and Soviet-backed rule while the antigovernment and anti-Soviet insurgency (eventually strongly backed and supplied by the United States) grew in strength and effectiveness. Bottom line: there were no peace treaties after the initial failure and none before the second failure in 1992. There was a UN peacekeeping mission that did begin in 1988 before the second failure—UNGOMAP (United Nations Good Offices Mission in Afghanistan and Pakistan). Still, there was no effective UN-based intervention, as the primary aim of UNGOMAP (a rather small mission with fewer than 150 military observers along with international and local civilian staff) was to facilitate Soviet withdrawal, and not provide a broader basis for stability.[16]

Guinea-Bissau

The single-failure Guinea-Bissau appears to be a case of a struggle to control government that spun out of control. As noted, Guinea-Bissau was rated as an anocracy before its failure (with a POLITY score of 5, putting it in a range we can call "almost democracy"). The political struggle quickly led to major armed civil violence, worsened by the government's invitation to neighboring countries to send troops, and generating large numbers of refugees. As noted in the 2010 POLITY IV Country Report for Guinea-Bissau, in most of the first decade of the twenty-first century the country "struggled to recover from the collapse of central governance following ex-President João Bernardo Vieira's attempt to remove his chief of staff, General Ansumane Mané, from office in June 1998."

In 1994 Vieira was elected president in Guinea-Bissau's first free election. On June 6, 1998, Vieira dismissed the suspended brigadier general Ansumane Mané as chief of staff, and appointed General Humberto Gomes to replace him. On June 7 Mané responded with an attempted coup d'état against the government of Vieira. Vieira's next move was to ask for military aid from neighboring Senegal and the Republic of Guinea. On June 10, thirteen hundred Senegalese and four hundred Guinean troops arrived. The internal conflict was then internationalized through invited intervention. As was later reported by the All Africa News Agency (August 3, 1998): "[T]he majority of the population is angry with the president for calling in foreign troops. People have to struggle to keep alive and they are all in revolt against the president. One of the reasons for the rebellion against Vieira is the lack of food and medicine."

On June 12 it was reported that more than forty thousand refugees had fled to Senegal before Senegal closed the border. Additionally, in order to stem the tide of refugees, on June 17 Senegalese troops fired heavy artillery into Guinea-Bissau. While the refugees from Guinea-Bissau expressed fear for their safety, Senegal claimed that it had fired into Guinea-Bissau in order to drive off its own separatist rebels, who were supporting Guinea-Bissau's coup leader Mané, and were also using Guinea-Bissau territory as a safe haven.

The extent of state breakdown was apparent by the end of June. Because of the level of fighting in Bissau, the capital and largest city in the country, many of its residents fled to escape the danger. However, they encountered the food and water shortages and fear of famine that were widespread outside of the capital. On July 4, 1998, ECOWAS announced its determination "to reassert the authority of that country's embattled president through a combination of negotiations, sanctions and the use of force, though they gave no specific details" (Associated press report). ECOWAS helped to establish a ceasefire between Vieira and the rebels that was broken in mid-October, causing a renewed flood of people fleeing the capital.

However, another ceasefire was signed on August 26 in Praia, Cape Verde. Under the auspices of ECOWAS the parties met in October and November in Abuja, Nigeria, completing the Agreement between the Government of Guinea Bissau and the Self-Proclaimed Military Junta, signed on November 1 by Vieira and Mané. The peace accord reaffirmed the August 26 ceasefire and called for the withdrawal of all foreign troops and the use of an ECOWAS "interposition" force to "guarantee security along the Guinea Bissau/Senegal border, keep the warring parties apart and guarantee free access to humanitarian organisations and agencies to reach the affected civilian population. In this regard, the Oswaldo Vieira international airport and the sea-port shall be opened immediately" (United States Institute of Peace Agreements Digital Collection).[17] This interposition force was ECOMOG (the ECOWAS Cease-fire Monitoring Group). The agreement also set a March 1999 data for elections, and created a Government of National Unity that would include members of the "Self-Proclaimed Junta."

In Guinea-Bissau, intervention by a regional organization, ECOWAS, was instrumental in managing the conflict. ECOWAS helped set up ceasefires, the last of which led directly to the November 1, 1998, peace accord, which it also brokered. It began its activities almost immediately after the civil war broke out and at the time of failure. The presence and activities of ECOMOG subsequent to the November 1 accord were effective, and were so praised by the United Nations.

External interventions may take a number of forms. The intervention by Senegal and Guinea was coded as "economic protective intervention" and "military/diplomacy protective intervention" by Kisangani and Pickering (2008). "Economic protective intervention" is where the "intervener attempts to protect economic or resource interests of self or others," while "intervention to protect own military and/or diplomatic interests and property inside or outside the target" refers to military property, diplomats, and/or diplomatic property. As Vieira was supported by only a minority of the military and his party, and Mané by most of the military and the major ethnic groups, the intervention by Senegal and Guinea was a major catalyst in that state failure. Indeed, what appears to be a relatively effective peace accord focused on removing these troops (a major factor in keeping Vieira in office) and relying on ECOWAS both to monitor the border with Senegal and to separate the internal warring factions.

The November 1 peace accord permitted the country to stabilize to the extent that the –77 coding ended in 1998, with a relatively stable constitutional government before the civil war reignited in 1999. In May 1999 Vieira was finally ousted by Mané, but there was no return to a –77 status. Indeed, despite continued conflict and problems in establishing democracy, the situation in Guinea-Bissau did not warrant a second collapse (U.S. Department of State Background Note: Guinea-Bissau, www.state.gov/r/pa/ei/bgn/).

DRC-Cambodia
Democratic Republic of the Congo

The story of the Congo (DRC) is a perfect storm of negligent and exploitative colonial rule, the departure of the colonial power leaving literally no sociopolitical infrastructure in place, all occurring within the context of Cold War competition as well as multiple regional/ethnic loyalties and separatist movements, leading to inflation, starvation, multiple armed conflicts, and anarchy. As noted earlier, there is no POLITY IV regime score before the 1962 failure as the country moved from colonial rule (in transition) directly to a –77 status.

The background to failure and the postfailure environment is complex, but we will produce a brief schematic. In 1960 Belgium held a roundtable conference with Congolese political leaders, agreeing on the future independence of the Congo after elections were held in May 1960. In May, the Mouvement National Congolais (MNC) Party, led by Patrice Lumumba, won the parliamentary elections. Lumumba was declared prime minister while Joseph Kasavubu was elected as president. The independent Republic of the Congo was declared on June 30, 1960.

In July 1960, the Republic of the Congo Army, lacking many native officers, mutinied against the white officers of the Leopoldville Garrison. This directly led to a military intervention by Belgium to rescue Belgian citizens and other foreigners. Most of the 100,000 Europeans who remained after independence fled at that time. In turn, Congolese now replaced European military and administrative elites. On July 11 the resource rich area of Katanga, led by Moise Tshombe and his CONAKAT Party (Confédération des associations tribales du Katanga) seceded from the Republic of Congo, revolting against the Lumumba government (Hales and Miller's [2010] "secession" trigger). The pro-Western Tshombe did so with the support of Belgian business interests and more than six thousand Belgian troops. As it was the richest and most developed part of the Congo, with its copper, gold, and uranium deposits, a successful secession would have been a major blow to the economic well-being of the Congo. While Tshombe repudiated the Marxist/communist line of Lumumba, the Congo government called the secession a Belgian attempt to set up a puppet government.

The UN Security Council approved Resolution 143 on July 14. This led to the creation of ONUC (Opération des Nations Unies au Congo), which by July 1961 had reached almost twenty thousand troops. According to the UN description of completed peacekeeping missions, "ONUC was established in July 1960 to ensure the withdrawal of Belgian forces, to assist the Government in maintaining law and order and to provide technical assistance. The function of ONUC was subsequently modified to include maintaining the territorial integrity and political independence of the Congo, preventing the occurrence of civil war and securing the removal of all foreign military, paramilitary and advisory personnel not under the United Nations Command, and all mercenaries."[18]

On August 8, 1960, South Kasai, a rich mining state, also seceded from the Congo, leading Lumumba to turn to the USSR for military aid. The USSR airlifted Congolese soldiers in and out of Kasai, undermining the UN's presence. In turn, on September 5 the United Nations closed all airports under their control, in effect stopping the Soviet airlift of troops. Only a week later, the army chief of staff, Joseph Mobutu, with the support of the U.S. government and with CIA assistance, placed Lumumba under house arrest, and in a military coup suspended parliament and the constitution. At the same time Lumumba's vice president created a rival government with its own military forces in Stanleyville.

We have now set the stage for the major internationalized civil conflict and state collapse that followed. By September 1960 there were, in effect, four different regimes in the Congo: (1) the regime led by Joseph Mobutu supported by Western governments in the capital of Leopoldville; (2) the regime led by Antoine Gizenga, former prime minister Lumumba's vice president, which had the support of the USSR in Stanleyville; (3) a regime in the seceded state of South Kasai; and (4) a regime in the other seceded state of Katanga, supported by Belgium and the mining companies.

The situation became more intense in December when Lumumba was captured by Mobutu forces, and first moved to Leopoldville. At some point he was transferred again, and on January 17, 1961, he was killed by Katangan forces. There was at this time a furious diplomatic interaction between the Soviets, the West, and the United Nations, particularly in the person of the secretary-general, Dag Hammarskjold. The UN Security Council adopted Resolution 161 in February, authorizing UN troops to use force against Katangan troops in order to prevent a civil war in the Congo by "any means necessary." UN forces then engaged in several operations against Katangan troops and mercenaries through 1961: Operation Rumpunch in August (which led to the expulsion of Belgian troops), and Operation Morthor in September, leading to open major battlefield operations against Katangan troops. Dag Hammarskjold died in a plane crash on September 17 on the way to negotiations with Tshombe and the Katanga forces. In December 1961 Congolese forces took back South Kasai, ending that secession. However, Katanga maintained its independence through 1962. Only in December 1962, after the United Nations had launched Operation Grand Slam, was there a decisive victory, taking Elizabethville (Katanga's capital) and ending the secession.

After the defeat of Katanga there were a succession of short-lived governments under Joseph Ileo, Cyrille Adoula, and Moise Tshombe, and tribal loyalties emerged as a major factor in the political struggles. The UN forces under ONUC were phased out by mid-1964 (with almost forty-nine hundred personnel at the time of withdrawal). In the Kisangani and Pickering data set (2008), ONUC was coded as "economic protective intervention," "strategic intervention," and "military/diplomatic intervention." Based on the PRIO/Uppsala data, there were no peace agreements signed after the first failure in 1962 or in the period up to the second failure in 1992. Thus, there were no agreements before the second collapse.

Returning to some of our opening comments—the DRC failed almost immediately after being given freedom from colonial rule. Indeed, a government was never really given the chance to stabilize before sections of the country attempted to secede (often backed by external forces). The new set of leaders (Kasavubu and Lumumba) never trusted each other, while Belgium (and the United States) financed and supported the army mutiny and the later military coup by Mobutu.

Mobutu was propped up by the U.S. until the end of the Cold War, when Zaire was no longer important to the Cold War struggle. Lack of U.S. support is one factor leading to the second occurrence of state failure. Both the dynamics of the first failure and the context of the second failure fit the classic "Cold War" explanation of global dynamics. The initial UN mission (essentially based on U.S. foreign policy) was there first to help push the Belgians out, and then to help deal with the secessionist movements, especially to quell the Katangan secession. UN forces were phased out after Katanga was reintegrated into the Congo. ONUC was a large and continuous action, but failed, and there were no peace treaties to form a structure for accommodation.

Cambodia

The case of Cambodia is another Cold War story. The disorder that occurred during a civil war between a military rule government and communist forces led to the brief –77 status, followed by years of heavily autocratic rule by a communist regime (in this case the term "totalitarian" is an apt one). In 1953 Cambodia received its independence from France, following Japanese occupation during World War II. Rule returned to Norodom Sihanouk, who had been king since 1941.

An early associate, Lon Nol, helped set up a right-wing monarchist proindependence party that was instrumental in helping Sihanouk in the 1955 elections. In the 1950s Lon Nol served as commander-in-chief of the armed forces and then defense minister, and became deputy premier in 1963. Even while Sihanouk followed an "extreme neutrality" policy during the Vietnam War, Lon Nol maintained ties to the United States. The 1966 elections saw a sharp rightist turn, and Lon Nol became prime minister. Sihanouk then used him and Cambodian army troops to repress a leftist rebellion in 1967.

In the midst of the Vietnam War, in March 1970, while Sihanouk was out of the country, anti-Vietnamese riots broke out. At that point Lon Nol and other military figures (the record is not quite clear who was leading whom) deposed Sihanouk as head of state, with the National Assembly formally stripping him of power. At that point, according to the Cambodia *Tribunal Monitor:*

> The Khmer Rouge [or the CPK—the Communist Party of Kampuchea] had gained members and was positioned to become a major player in the civil war .... Their army was led by Pol Pot, who was appointed CPK's party secretary and leader in 1963 .... Aided by the Vietnamese, the Khmer Rouge began to defeat Lon Nol's forces on the battlefields. By the end of 1972, the Vietnamese withdrew from Cambodia and turned the major responsibilities for the war over to the CPK. From January to August 1973, the [Cambodian government], with assistance from the United States, dropped about half a million tons of bombs on Cambodia, which may have killed as many as 300,000 people. Many who resented the bombings or had lost family members joined the Khmer Rouge's revolution. By early 1973, about 85 percent of Cambodian territory was in the hands of the Khmer Rouge, and the Lon Nol army was almost unable to go on the offensive. However, with US assistance, it was able to continue fighting the Khmer Rouge for two more years.

As the United States prepared to withdraw the last of its forces from Vietnam, and following Lon Nol's departure from Cambodia on April 1, Khmer Rouge units took Phnom Penh on April 17, 1975 (the U.S. would evacuate the last of its personnel from Saigon on April 30). The fall of Phnom Penh marked the end to five years of civil war between the rightist government that deposed Sihanouk in 1970 and the Khmer Rouge, and major foreign interventions by both the United States and North Vietnam, which included the massive bombing.

What occurred next is briefly summarized by the CIA World Factbook:

> In April 1975, after a five-year struggle, Communist Khmer Rouge forces captured Phnom Penh and evacuated all cities and towns. At least 1.5 million Cambodians died from execution, forced hardships, or starvation during the Khmer Rouge regime under Pol Pot. A December 1978 Vietnamese invasion drove the Khmer Rouge into the countryside, began a 10-year Vietnamese occupation, and touched off almost 13 years of civil war.

This is key for the present discussion, because it helps explain the absence of a second failure. The totalitarian autocracy established under the Khmer Rouge ruled with the proverbial iron hand until the Vietnamese invasion. While its policies wreaked havoc on Cambodian society and caused massive democide (in Rummel's terms), the Khmer Rouge was in full control. It was an auto-cratic and murderous state, but not a failed one. With the Vietnamese victory, Cambodia could well be considered a –66. However it might have been coded, it was not –77. Despite the Vietnamese having to fight a war of occupation, the country never descended into chaos.

Peace negotiations began in 1989, along with other sea changes in the com-munist world. It was only in October 1991, with the Paris Agreement, that there had been any peace treaty, or any UN peacekeeping mission.[19] The presence of UNAMIC (United Nations Advance Mission in Cambodia), which lasted from October 1991 until March 1992, appeared to be able to help stabilize the situa-tion in the short term. Importantly, it was followed by UNTAC (United Nations Transitional Authority in Cambodia), beginning in February 1992 (and lasting until September 1993). UNTAC's mandate was set forth as:

> UNTAC was established to ensure implementation of the Agreements on the Com-prehensive Political Settlement of the Cambodia Conflict, signed in Paris on 23 Oc-tober 1991. The mandate included aspects relating to human rights, the organization and conduct of elections, military arrangements, civil administration, maintenance of law and order, repatriation and resettlement of refugees and displaced persons and rehabilitation of Cambodian infrastructure."[20]

Again, attending to the Cambodian infrastructure and other state-building measures may have been the key factor in staving off a recurrence of a second failure. Indeed, in an article written not long after the Paris Agreement, Helman and Ratner (1992–93) argue the need for several different forms of "conserva-torship" to be pursued by the United Nations to aid failed or failing countries. They note:

> For those states that have already failed, a second, more intrusive form of conserva-torship would be appropriate. Here, the state could actually delegate certain govern-mental functions to the U.N. That process is already underway, at least in theory, in Cambodia, which clearly qualifies as a failed state: Twenty years of civil war, inva-sions, outside arms supplies, gross violations of human rights, massive dislocations of its population, and destruction of its infra-structure have rendered the country incapable of governing itself. (1992–93, 14)

They point out that UNTAC was set up essentially to control five ministries and supervise others. Thus, despite all the conditions discussed above and listed by Helman and Ratner, Cambodia did not fail again.

Ethiopia-Uganda

Ethiopia

Unlike the DRC and the Ivory Coast, Ethiopia was free of colonial rule, except for a brief period of Italian occupation in 1935. Haile Selassie, who had become emperor in 1930, was restored to rule by the British in 1941. He remained in power until 1974, the year for which Ethiopia was coded as a –77. However, as with the DRC and Afghanistan, the conflict in Ethiopia took place within the Cold War struggle between governments that were traditional or West-leaning, and some form of communist/Marxist opposition groups. In the case of Ethiopia, the Cold War context worsened a situation that involved a major separatist movement, discontent in the military, and severe conditions of drought and famine.

A famine in 1973, brought on by a drought that affected 2 million farmers in northern Ethiopia, had killed tens of thousands of people. The drought had spread to areas in the east and south of Ethiopia in 1974. Despite international relief efforts, which were to be stretched even further, government plans, programs, and understanding of the problem appeared inadequate, and many experts feared that there would be more such deaths. In some areas of the country the perception was that the government response (or lack thereof) to famine conditions was consciously callous, as food was still being exported. A great deal of discontent was generated by social and regional divisions within the country, best personified by the Eritrean Liberation Front, which had begun armed struggle in the early 1960s to establish an independent Eritrea—an armed separatist movement that continued throughout this period.

In early 1974 segments of the military protested against low pay, and joined protests by students, teachers, and others in a general strike over inflation, unemployment, and the famine. An army mutiny in Asmara, the country's second largest city, continued to erode Haile Selassie's authority despite a number of concessions. The emperor had accepted the resignation of the government, announced pay raises, and promised constitutional reform. He also appointed a new prime minister, who formed a cabinet composed of "enlightened" members of the traditional nobility and, in addition, "technocrats" of limited administrative experience. The pay raises were implemented for both the military and civilian workers, despite government claims that they could not be afforded. With its inflationary effects (prices on many staples had risen 80 percent or more), the government moved to new economic austerity measures. The increase in world oil prices also had a negative impact on any government actions, which did nothing to quell the spreading mutiny in the north, where the army and police threatened action over the government's failure to make social and political reforms, especially in the area of corruption.

In late June of 1974, army troops imposed a curfew in Addis Ababa, and essentially took control of the country without actually staging a coup, but rather forming an Armed Forces Coordinating Committee known as the Dergue (or Derg). The committee's declared goal was unity, despite tribal and class distinctions throughout the country, and an "Ethiopia First" policy. However, many members were Marxists, and the Dergue took on the form of a radical Marxist government. Mengistu Haile Mariam was made the chairman of the Armed Forces Coordinating Committee. On September 12, 1974, Haile Selassie was formally deposed, along with the proclamation of a Provisional Military Administrative Council (PMAC), run by the Dergue, and which assumed the role of government.

Mengistu was made vice chairman of the PMAC but soon rose as its strongman (reportedly engineering the murder of other PMAC members as well as numerous individuals in the former government). The PMAC did announce in late November 1974 that they had executed sixty former government official and cabinet members (among two hundred former government officials being held on charges of corruption and malfeasance). In late December 1974 the military government declared its intention to turn Ethiopia into a socialist country with a one-party system, government control of all property needed for economic progress, and collective farms, with the overall aim to modernize the traditional and largely agricultural country.

The Ethiopian case can be summarized as follows. The civil war was intensified because of drought and famine. Neighboring countries were unable to provide any aid or support because they were suffering from the same circumstances. The new government in Ethiopia was socialist, and became more radically Marxist—and was later ousted during Ethiopia's second period of state failure. This government did not allow the democratic freedoms that some other African countries enacted after their own state failure.

Additionally, there was no peace agreement signed after the first failure. Nor was there one after the second failure, which occurred in 1991, the same year as the war against Eritrea ended. While at various times from 1974 to 1991 there was an internationalization of violence with interventions from Cuba, Russia, and Somalia, there were no regional or UN-based peacekeeping operations.

Thus there was no help from the United Nations or other IGOs, only a worsened military situation in region as a whole.

Uganda

In Uganda we find a story of factional civil war taking place within a context created by authoritarian rule, multiple ethnic groups, border wars with Kenya and Tanzania, and conflict and unrest in neighboring states (which were suffering from drought and famine and which also generated large numbers of refugees moving into Uganda). A brief overview is provided by the 2010 POLITY IV Country Report:

> Political instability and authoritarian rule have long defined politics in Uganda. After a brief struggle between federal and tribal authorities in the early independence years, the 1966 coup by Prime Minister Obote centralized political authority and ushered in a system of one-party rule. Obote's rule was interrupted in 1971 when Major General Idi Amin seized power in a military coup. President Amin's bloody tenure in office was abruptly ended in 1979 when the Ugandan National Liberation Army, with the active support of Tanzanian troops, forced Amin to flee the country. After a series of short-lived provisional governments and yet another coup, legislative elections were held in 1980. In these elections, which were marred by significant irregularities, Obote's Ugandan People's Congress party won a majority of seats in the National Assembly and Obote was subsequently proclaimed president of Uganda. In response to the fraudulent nature of these elections, three guerrilla movements organized an effort to unseat President Obote. Yoweri Museveni led the largest of the three guerrilla organizations, the National Resistance Army (NRA).

Increasing human rights violations and deepening fissures within the military between its two main ethnic factions (Acholi and Langi) marred President Obote's rule during the early 1980s. In the summer of 1985 these factional struggles erupted into open warfare and Obote was forced to flee the country By July 1985 Uganda under Obote faced charges of massive human rights abuses, was enmeshed in insurgencies and insurgent terrorism, and had stopped taking money from the IMF. Neighboring Sudan had suffered a military coup, and refuges from several countries were adding to Uganda's problems. At the same time that the various guerrilla groups were making advances against Obote, there was a tribal split in the Ugandan army, with mutinous sections moving to home areas (such as General Tito Okello moving to his home area in the north). Fighting throughout the country occurred across regional, ethnic, and religious lines.

On July 28, 1985, President Obote was formally ousted and replaced by a military regime headed by Okello. This regime, however, was beset by factionalism from both within the military and throughout society. Civil unrest, especially in the capital of Kampala, also indicated the fragility of the Okello government. From this point until the end of the year, a political vacuum grew along with growing anarchy. The different factions in the military and the guerrilla organizations engaged in peace talks presided over by a Kenyan delegation under Kenyan president Daniel Arap Moi that lasted from August until mid-December. A ceasefire was agreed upon, but the difficulty and bitterness of the negotiations were demonstrated by its immediate breakdown. Museveni and the NRA (and its allies) felt that they could win on their own.

This victory was made more difficult when, in late January, hundreds of Ugandan troops loyal to Idi Amin, and who had been secretly training in Zaire (DRC) with the blessing of Mobutu Sese Seko, moved into Uganda along with Zairean military personnel. However, Museveni prevailed, and on January 25, his NRA troops took Kampala and ousted Okello. When sworn in as president on January 29, 1986, Museveni declared: "This is not a mere change of guard, it is a fundamental change .... The people of Africa, the people of Uganda, are entitled to a democratic government. It is not a favour from any regime. The sovereign people must be the public, not the government."[21]

The primary challenge that Ugandan leaders had faced since independence was pulling together all of the tribes/ethnic groups within Uganda. As briefly noted above, this resulted in a long history of violence, repression, and human rights abuses. The Museveni government, installed by the NRA toward the end of the Ugandan failed state period, appears to have welcomed diversity and fought for human rights. Museveni told foreign diplomats that he would be committed to protecting human rights. In July 1986 he established an office to combat government corruption. Throughout 1986 there were reports that refugees who had fled Uganda under previous regimes had returned. Local government reform gave tribes more voice in local affairs. Signs of an improving economy began in 1986, deriving in part from a rise in export prices and foreign aid. Many observers of the Museveni/NRA government have been positive about the record on civil rights abuses, economic and political reforms, including work with the IMF, the World Bank, and other donors regarding foreign aid.

All of this appears to be important regarding the avoidance of a second state failure. Despite another case of "complex" conflict, greater democracy, legitimacy through performance, and the use of international organizations appear to help distinguish Uganda from Ethiopia. This is particularly important given the continuing insurgency of the Lord's Resistance Army (LRA) and other groups. In 2002 the Yumbe Peace Agreement was concluded with the UN-RFII (the Uganda National Rescue Front). Peace agreements were negotiated with the LRA in spring/summer 2007, as well as February 2008. The Museveni government also supported the OAU in sending peacekeeping forces to monitor the Uganda-Rwanda border in 1992 (under NMOG I, the Neutral Military Observer Group). This also applied to peacekeeping missions from the United Nations in 1993 and 1994 for the same purpose (UNOMUR, UN Observer Mission Uganda-Rwanda; and UNOMIR, UN Assistance Mission for Rwanda). UNAMIR was created to implement and monitor agreements regarding Rwanda and support its transitional government, thus reducing regional violence that could spill into/involve Uganda. These sorts of activities reflect a general attempt to control conflict, to create agreements for ceasefires, and to monitor them as well as troop movements. Given the set of causes for state failure, Uganda appears to be instructive as to how to avoid a future failure.

Ivory Coast–Solomon Islands

Ivory Coast

The final set of matched cases is that of the Ivory Coast and the Solomon Islands. This comparison is important in that it is the only set of matched cases in which both of the failures in the Ivory Coast, and the single failure in the Solomon Islands occurred after 1989 and the end of the Cold War. For our first matched pair, Afghanistan/Guinea-Bissau, the Cold War context, and the dynamics of U.S.-Soviet competition, had a substantial impact on the initial failure in Afghanistan, adding a major international interventionist component to the very high levels of conflict. The same is true of both the DRC and Cambodia in their matched pair. The DRC was a textbook case of the effects of combined internal and external conflict, with substantial external interventions. In the first failure of the DRC, the Cold War context was central. The Cold War context was related to the Cambodian failure only in that the withdrawal of U.S. forces from Vietnam created the vacuum and provided the opportunity for conflict that brought the Khmer Rouge to power. The Ethiopian failure in 1974 had certain parallels with Cambodia—conflict between monarchical governments and hard line communist insurgent movements. In both cases the communist opposition, the Khmer Rouge and the Derg, emerged victorious. And, like single-failure Cambodia, while Ethiopia was ruled by ruthless, hardcore autocratic communist regimes, there was no failure, which came only after that regime had ended. As we shall see, both the Ivory Coast and the Solomon Islands suffered state failure under quite different global conditions.

The story in the Ivory Coast was one of the politics of autocracy and political survival. As described in the POLITY IV Country Report: "Between 1960 and 1990 a small clan of elite politicians maintained a remarkable degree of political stability in Cote d'Ivoire, at least for African standards, by playing musical chairs with key government posts and by dealing with the political opposition through a combination of state patronage and government repression." Although there was some political liberalization following student-led demonstrations in 1990, the one-party rule by founding president Felix Houphouet-Boigny and his Democratic Party of Cote d'Ivoire (PDCI) continued after his death in 1993 until the late 1990s. When PDCI president Henri Konan Bedie tried to rig the 2000 election, massive protests in 1999 led to the Ivory Coast's first military coup. When General Guei attempted the same electoral manipulation, more massive demonstrations forced him to cede the 2000 election to Laurent Gbagbo. Gbagbo drew support from large numbers of the country's youth angry about economic conditions—and following the line of Bedie and Guei—blaming the decline on migrants from other parts of West Africa who first came to work on, and then own, large areas of choice cocoa-growing land.

Gbagbo spent a good deal of his efforts attempting to appease the military, but a successful military mutiny took control of much of the northern half of the country in 2002, when rebels angry at the exclusion of their candidate from the presidential election tried to push Mr. Gbagbo from power. The Ivory Coast had been divided between the rebel-controlled, largely Muslim north and the government-controlled south since 2002.[22] This highlights the important place of ethnic conflict in the Ivory Coast. In addition to blaming immigrants, Ivorian government leaders have also used the ethnic card to secure their hold on power, especially as economic conditions worsened in the late 1990s. According to POLITY IV, "Ethnicity [with four major and more than 60 minor ethnic groups] became an increasingly volatile and divisive issue in this country. The country's civil war, ostensibly to right the wrongs associated with citizenship rules, reflects the ethnic diversity issue." In terms that resonate with the selectorate-based political survival model (Bueno de Mesquita et al. 2003), POLITY IV notes: "President Houphouet-Boigny was able to keep the 'tribalization' of his country at bay by distributing state patronage widely amongst all ethnic groups."

Another significant part of the story of the Ivory Coast has been serious civil conflict, involving military peacekeeping missions by both ECOWAS and the

United Nations. The first peacekeeping mission was sponsored by ECOWAS in October 2002, deploying ECOMICI with 2,386 men contributed by eight ECOWAS members. ECOMICI's mandate was to monitor the cessation of hostilities; facilitate the return of normal public administrative services and the free movement of goods and services; contribute to the implementation of the peace agreement; and guarantee the safety of the insurgents, observers, and humanitarian staff. However, ECOWAS pledged troops they could not commit and was far too understaffed to fulfill the mandate's four components or phases. ECOMICI (which ran from October 2002 until April 2004) stopped at the first phase, simply monitoring the ceasefire zone.

The ECOWAS mission was joined by the United Nations Mission in Cote d'Ivoire (MINUCI) in June 2003 (ending in April 2004). MINUCI was composed of up to seventy-five military observers and fifty-five civilian personnel. In October 2003 an ECOWAS delegation to the United Nations asked for help to increase ECOMICI strength, and to turn it into a UN peacekeeping force. MINUCI ended in April 2004 and was replaced at that time by the United Nations Operation in Cote d'Ivore (UNOCI). Originally staffed with almost seven thousand uniformed personnel, it remains in the Ivory Coast to this day. Its mandate was a broad one (with thirteen major components) and was to be accomplished in cooperation with the French forces stationed in the Ivory Coast.[23]

The case of the Ivory Coast has also been characterized by a series of ineffective peace agreements both before the 2006 failure, and between 2006 and the 2010 failure. As POLITY IV notes: "In January 2003 President Gbagbo accepted a peace deal which proposed the formation of a power-sharing government of national unity. The government of national unity would consist of Gbagbo and his followers as well as representatives from the G7 (the three rebel factions plus the four main opposition political parties) .... One year after the signing of the Linas-Marcoussis Peace Agreement in Paris in January 2003, the fighting had stopped but the country remained deeply divided and reconciliation continued to be an elusive ideal." Indeed, in September 2003 the New Forces left the Government of National Reconciliation created by the Linas-Marcoussis Agreement, and by the end of 2004 the peace agreement was falling apart.

One element in the failure of the agreement was French involvement (indeed, French control was seen as an element in the 1999 conflict and coup). ECOWAS was held in suspicion as being a tool of the French, and French peacekeeping forces (initially sent under the auspices of the 1961 defense agreement between France and the Ivory Coast) were often the targets of the armed opposition groups. In November 2004, after an incident that killed nine French peace-keepers, "[t]he renewed violence triggered political instability in the capital of Abidjan. French troops restored peace to the capital city and, in the process, destroyed almost the entire Ivorian air force in retaliation for the killing of its peacekeepers in Bouake. Led by Gbagbo's Young Patriots Militia, anti-French demonstrations subsequently engulfed the capital resulting in fifty-seven dead, 2,000 injured and over 9,000 French residents displaced" (POLITY IV).

A transitional government ultimately was established in 2005, but it took all of 2006 to work out the Ouagadougou Peace Agreement in March 2007 (with the assistance of President Compaore of Burkina Faso). The agreement set out a power-sharing settlement between the government and the New Forces. The second failure was triggered in 2010 when President Gbagbo dissolved the government and the electoral commission, then relented to allow November elections. POLITY IV reports: "[T]he presidential elections held on 28 November 2010 unleashed a political crisis that divided the country once again into rival territories enforced by ethnic militias: the north and west supported Ouattara and recognized his victory in the presidential election, while the southeast continued to support Gbagbo and his refusal to cede executive authority." International mediation failed; conflict and civil war broke out again.[24]

The Ivory Coast appears to be a case of ineffective peacekeeping and the breakdown of agreements. As noted, there were peacekeeping missions prior to first collapse—but their presence did not help; while the UN and French missions continued, they did not avert a second collapse. Regarding peace agreements, there was one in 2003 and another before the first collapse, the Pretoria Agreement on the Peace Process in Cote d'Ivoire (April 2005). Following the 2006 failure, there were four additional peace agreements, the Ouagadougou Political Agreement in March 2007 being the first. This was followed by three other agreements: the First Complementary Agreement to Ouagadougou (also in March 2007), then the Second and Third in November 2007, and the Fourth in December 2008. Yet neither peacekeeping missions nor treaties prevented the second failure in 2010. The second failure, as noted, was also triggered by elections (which are another item in Hales and Miller's 2010 list of state failure triggers, supporting the observation of Fearon and Laitin, noted above).

Solomon Islands

The story in the Solomon Islands is one of dealing with poor government performance ("personalistic politics" in a weak party system, according to POL-

ITY IV), within the context of significant ethnic division and major economic difficulties. The level of militarized and lethal civil conflict was quite low, and minimized by effective ceasefires. A regional peacekeeping intervention beginning in 2003 (Regional Assistance Mission to Solomon Islands: RAMSI) funded by, and led by, Australia and New Zealand for the Pacific Islands Forum appears to have been effective.

The source of the ethnic tensions underlying conflict in the Solomon Islands is the relationship between the Malaita Islanders (a group brought to the islands by the United States in World War II to help drive out the Japanese) and the native Isatabu. The Malaita remained and were active both economically and politically, especially around the capital of Honiara. This was strongly resented by the native Isatabu Islanders (local name for Guadalcanal), and landownership rights became a major issue. As POLITY IV notes, the Isatabu "mobilized their resentment in the 1990s and demanded special compensation from the central government for hosting the capital. When that was denied [under the government of Prime Minister Bartholomew Ulufa'alu, who was elected in 1997] local militias (Isatabu Freedom Fighters) were formed to intimidate and drive Malaitans out of the island. Many Malaitans fled to Honiara and a militant group formed to protect them: the Malaita Eagles Force (MEF). Clashes between the militias in the late 1990s culminated in a MEF seizure of the capital on 5 June 2000, and the forced resignation of Prime Minister Ulufa'alu." While conflict was managed with agreements in 2000 and 2001, it once again turned violent in 2002 and was "followed by a prevailing atmosphere of lawlessness and ineffective rule of law" (POLITY IV).

This context of ethnic conflict was exacerbated by poor economic and governmental performance. In 2002 public debt had ballooned (with the national debt doubling in a year), and government plans to downsize the public sector by 40 percent were strongly opposed by the Solomon Islands Public Employees Union (SIPEU). While law and order problems mounted, a governmentsponsored "weapons and stolen property amnesty" program was repeatedly extended, but to little effect except to promote violence. While the decline in world commodity prices on the country's major exports (in agriculture, fisheries, mining, oil palm, forestry, and copra) as well as the Asian monetary crisis of the late 1990s contributed to the economic problems of the Solomon Islands, these were exacerbated by poor fiscal management and the absence of macroeconomic policies. Poor government performance was highlighted by steady inflation, the closing down of government services in health and education, the clash with public unions, and the government's inability to meet public salaries. Both internal and external observers also noted that some government services, especially the police, were highly corrupt. A useful way to summarize this is from an article from the SIBC (Solomon Islands Broadcasting Corporation): "An International Monetary Fund IMF and Civil Society Network meeting this morning agreed that the government needs to take firmer action to turn the economy around. They have also stressed that the compensation money payments be stopped and that government strongly exercises accountability, good governance and transparency."[25]

With violence increasing and governmental control breaking down, the Solomon Islands prime minister, Sir Allan Kemakeza, requested assistance from the regional Pacific Islands Forum in April 2003, flying to Canberra in June to receive the PIF offer of assistance in the form of RAMSI. According to the RAMSI website:

> After five years of ethnic tensions, and a coup in 2000, the problems facing his troubled nation were many and serious .... Law and order had broken down, officials and private citizens were subject to intimidation and violence, and corruption was unfettered. The Government and its institutions had ceased to function effectively. Corruption was widespread. Public finances were in ruin and many of the most basic services such as health and education were not being delivered to the people .... On 22 July 2003, the Solomon Islands National Parliament unanimously passed the Facilitation of International Assistance Act 2003, which provides authority under Solomon Islands domestic law for RAMSI's activities.[26]

RAMSI was thus seen as a partnership between the Solomon Islands and the fifteen members of the PIF, led by Australia and New Zealand. Its mandate included the following: ensure the safety and security of Solomon Islands; repair and reform the machinery of government, improve government accountability, and improve the delivery of services in urban and provincial areas; improve economic governance and strengthen the government's financial systems; help rebuild the economy and encourage sustainable broad-based growth; and build strong and peaceful communities. This mandate was to be achieved by 450 personnel working through three components: the Participating Police Force (PPF), the military Combined Task Force (CTF, including personnel from Australia, New Zealand, Tonga, and Papua New Guinea), and a civilian component that includes in-line personnel and advisors placed in key government agencies. This last component is perhaps the most important factor in comparing the matched cases, the peacekeeping mission being both a partnership and one with a central civilian component.

In sum, the level of violent conflict seen here is substantially lower than in the Ivory Coast or the other three double-failures. The regional peacekeeping mission had a significant civilian component and a central set of institution-building mandates. Without contiguous borders, there were no external interventions to worsen the problem. Despite continuing problems, with a much more solid democratic basis, all of these factors appear to be enough to prevent a second "collapse." Using data from PRIO/Uppsala we see that there were no peace agreements after the 2002 failure, with low levels of violence (actually no real civil war/rebellion that would require such an agreement). The issues of corruption, governmental performance (especially economic), and the failure of institutions were and continued to be addressed by the RAMSI intervention. Having no real major internal armed violence (that is, civil wars/rebellions) apparently helps a good deal!

CONCLUSION

Several broad directions for further investigation regarding the recurrence of state failure have been generated by the analysis of the matched cases. Esty et al. (1998) in their analyses of Political Instability Task Force (PITF) data (see also Hales and Miller 2010, 1) noted three important predictor variables to state failure in two years: international trade openness, infant mortality, and level of democracy. We have used all three variables in our Chapter Three analyses, and here as comparative factors across the eight cases.

Just as the causes of state failure have a major conflictual component, we find that for three of the double-failure cases, the level of conflict following the first failure was very high, and at a level substantially higher than the matched cases. The exception was the double-failure case of the Ivory Coast, the only post–Cold War double-failure. While avoiding the ideological and strategic overlay of the Cold War, it was still characterized by the ethnic components that were part of, and exacerbated, the conflict in the other three double-failures.

Classic issues in the study of development—urban-rural distinctions and conflict, patronage, corruption, kleptocracy, and tribalism—appear to be related to ethnic issues and also contributed not only to the high levels of conflict but also perceptions of poor governmental performance and lack of legitimacy. In addition, all of these factors were related to some aspect of the political survival model, and the size and nature of the selectorate, as well as the existence of large amounts of "free goods" (again see Bueno de Mesquita and Smith 2009b or Smith 2008). A more complete discussion of the linkages among these factors is found in Bates (2008), who traces the relationship of the costs of patronage to a movement from multiparty systems to single-party systems in Africa. This movement toward autocracy was also related to the ethnic support needed for political survival. In sum, such internal factors are clearly contributory to failure, and possibly repeated failure, but have not as yet been demonstrated to be necessary conditions. As Rotberg (2003, 5) notes: "There is no failed state without disharmonies between communities. Yet, the simple fact that many weak nation-states include haves and have-nots, and that some of the newer states contain a heterogeneous array of ethnic, religious, and linguistic interests, is more a contributor to than a root cause of nation-state failure."

As such, it also appears that as higher levels of democracy reduce the risk of the onset of state failure, they also have a dampening effect on the recurrence of state failure. Overall, the single-failure cases were further along the POLITY scale toward democracy at the time of the first failure than were the double-failure cases. Three of the single-failure matches were POLITY rated anocracies, and one a democracy. Interestingly, this finding stands against the common view that anocracies (or the Partially Free states in the Freedom House data) are more unstable and are more liable to civil war, because they lack the stabilizing effects found in either recognized democracies or strong autocracies. Keep in mind, however, that these higher scores toward the democratic end did not stop the matched cases from the first failure, but only that they appear to be a factor in preventing a second failure. In the double-failure cases, strong autocracies either prevented a second failure (as in single-failure Cambodia), or postponed second failures until major internal and external conflict in a post–Cold War environment overwhelmed them: the DRC and Ethiopia; internal conflict only in Afghanistan. For Afghanistan (as well as single-failure Cambodia), the situation after the first failure was closer to a –66 situation.

Democracy was also seen as part of a network of linkages to other states and IGOs that could make other actors in the global system both aware of and concerned about the dangers of a second failure. We found IGO memberships, economic organization memberships, and degree of economic integration stronger for the single-failure matched cases as well. There were also indications that the right sort of foreign aid could also help avoid second failures. On the other hand, however, as in the previous chapter, the role of economic upturns in keeping states from failing does not appear to be a factor. Indeed, the full role of economic measures seems to be complicated by the dynamics of political survival, especially in keeping the support and loyalty of relatively small selectorates and winning coalitions. The double-failure cases in particular illustrated the negative synergies among ethnic, tribal, and regional factors with small selectorates, and military coups or insurgencies.

IGO membership could not only reflect linkages to the international system, but have important effects on conflict management. Above we discussed the impact of economic regional organizations. Research by Karreth and Tir (2013) has similarly shown that "highly structured intergovernmental organizations" (HSIGOs) can help manage conflict within member states, particularly the escalation of internal conflict to civil war. They do this through mitigating "an important aspect of uncertainty associated with bargaining failure, including enhancing the credibility of commitments" (Karreth and Tir 2013, 96).

Another aspect of external linkages that is directly related to conflict management involves the presence and role of peacekeeping missions/interventions (see, for example, Schultz 2010; and Rost and Grieg 2011).[27] Only two of the double-failure cases had some form of regional and/or UN intervention during and immediately after the first collapse. Afghanistan did have UN missions before the second collapse. Ethiopia had activity only after the second failure. The DRC had multiple and substantial UN activity before and during the first collapse, but none before the second collapse; however, there was substantial activity after the DRC's second failure. The Ivory Coast had both regional West African and UN activity before the first collapse, much of which continued up through the second collapse in 2010.

We do find some possible evidence on the use and effectiveness of peacekeeping interventions when we contrast each double-failure with its matched case. While two of the double-failures had no attempts by regional or UN groups to help handle the conflicts, two did. All four of the single-failures did. Even Cambodia actually fits in the pattern of the other three single-failures: assistance coming in closely after the failure. Cambodia and Uganda were similar in that the UN missions appeared to be effective in three key areas: monitoring, enforcing, and focusing attention on previous cease-fires or conflict management agreements. These conclusions seem to support the findings of Beardsley's (2011) large-N analyses. He reviews literature which demonstrates that peacekeeping can prevent conflict recurrence. His analyses indicate that peacekeeping also reduces the risk that conflict will spread. In part, he concludes (2011, 1051): "One of the key means by which peacekeeping helps contain conflict is through addressing problems related to transnational movement of and support for insurgencies, thereby specifically preventing intrastate conflict from increasing the propensity for new intrastate conflict nearby." We noted that this was an obvious factor in regard to the single-failure Solomon Islands.

A second conflict management mechanism is the presence or absence of peace treaties between warring parties, whether they consist of a government and internal opposition groups or state-to-state relations. In searching for the effects of peace treaties, we are reflecting extant efforts to look at the management and resolution of conflict over territorial disputes, and the differential effects across a range of agreements/treaties (see, for example, Hartzell et al. 2001; Hensel et al. 2006; Simmons 2002). In general, agreements that are monitored (usually by some form of peacekeeping mission) appear to have a conflict-dampening effect for the postfailure period of single-failure cases. Our cases thus seem to support Schultz (2010), who finds that peace agreements with monitoring provisions tend to have more positive results.[28] Overall, our findings also support a conclusion by Blair and Fitz-Gerald (2009, 12) in their review of British policy to bring about "stabilisation," that "effective statebuilding is perhaps the central priority in stabilisation and needs to be understood in three dimensions: achieving a political settlement that incorporates the interests of the main power and interest groups; putting into place the state's 'survival functions'—security, the rule of law and taxation; and being able in some measure to meet citizens' expectations on the availability of basic services" (see also Mattes and Savun 2009).

While many internal issues need to be attended to in order to avoid a second failure, these external linkages and conflict management techniques appear to be necessary. In discussing the importance of studying state failure in Chapter One we raised important issues regarding the neighbor, region, and global effects generated by state failure—or, in short, issues of "order." Order, in turn, can clearly be analyzed as a collective good (for example, see Starr 1997). As such, we can say that the title of one of the earliest discussions of collective goods in international relations by Norman Frohlich and Joe Oppenheimer (1970) is particularly pertinent to the recurrence of failed states: "I Get By with a Little Help from My Friends."

6   The Consequences of State Failure

INTRODUCTION

State failure reflects the collapse of a sovereign state, and has been hypothesized to destabilize an entire region. In this chapter, we assess the negative effects of state collapse, with particular attention to the spatial diffusion of these consequences.[1] We argue that the instability, unrest, and civil war that increase the hazard of state collapse are not limited to the failed/collapsed state; states neighboring—or located within close distance of—a failed state are also likely to experience subsequently higher levels of political instability, unrest, civil war, and interstate conflict. We also evaluate the likelihood of state failure itself diffusing to other states. Specifically, we test the proposition that state failure causes political turmoil in close-by states to a greater extent than in distant countries. We do so by including a distance-weighted measure of state failure and by evaluating the effect of collapse in contiguous states. We conclude that state failure/collapse itself is not contagious, but some of its most negative consequences do indeed diffuse to other states.

The issue of "failed" states, including the negative consequences of state failure, has drawn significant attention from a number of international actors. This is because failed states are seen as being linked to a range of problems—economic, social, political, and military. They are associated with a wide range of negative consequences for their own populations, their neighbors, their regions, and the global community. The concern within academic as well as policy-making circles about the collapse of weak states is to a great extent due to the possible negative impact of such occurrences at the international (or regional) level. In this chapter, we examine the likelihood of regional diffusion of state collapse and the key negative consequences of state failure, including political instability and civil and interstate war. Specifically, we argue that failure in a state leads to destabilizing effects in neighboring and nearby states.

State failure may result in political disturbances ranging from minor political unrest to interstate war. Of concern here is the question whether these effects of state failure spread to neighboring states, and whether states in close proximity of a failed state have a higher likelihood of experiencing a collapse. The consequences of state collapse we study include political unrest and instability, civil war, international conflict, and state failure itself. Numerous studies over the past forty years have shown that the causes of violent conflict—both external and domestic—include previous violent conflict. Conflict has been found to act as both cause and consequence of further conflict. Similarly, we consider state failure, and its effects, as both a consequence and cause of further state failure. Discovering evidence of whether state failure and its effects diffuse, and to what extent, is central to policy questions of how to deal with state failure.

DIFFUSION/CONTAGION AND STATE FAILURE

In general, and as noted in the first chapter, the analysis of state failure can be seen as an exercise in policy evaluation. Previous investigators, as noted, have considered this a dangerous phenomenon, with dire consequences. Working from this belief, policy prescriptions have been made in order to forestall such negative consequences. However, before we can have much confidence in such policy prescriptions, we have argued that a number of analytic tasks must be undertaken. Chapter Three identified a set of key factors or conditions that increase the probability that a state will "fail." These factors include political instability, domestic unrest, civil war, and international conflict. That analysis revealed that both civil war and international conflict increase the likelihood of state failure, with civil war displaying a significantly stronger impact. Measures of lower levels of political upheaval at the domestic level—political instability and unrest—were also positively associated with state collapse. A central question here is whether the factors associated with causing state failure—instability, unrest, civil war, and international conflict, as well as state failure itself—lead to similar conditions in neighboring and nearby states. We can thus evaluate whether state failure has the negative consequences that more anecdotal/less rigorous analyses have suggested.

The negative consequences of state failure noted above would result from the working of some sort of diffusion processes. Most and Starr (1980) open their article on diffusion, reinforcement, and the spread of conflict by noting that the "notion that an event may alter the probability of subsequent events through diffusion or contagion processes is not new" (932). While three decades ago there were relatively few researchers studying diffusion, the application of spatial diffusion or contagion models has become far more common, even if only implicitly referenced through the use of contiguity as an independent, intervening, or control variable. The interest in the impact of geography and location of states on various issues in international relations continues to grow (see, for example, Beck et al. 2006; Gleditsch and Ward 2002; Simmons and Elkins 2004; see also the overview in Starr 2013). The diffusion approach itself reflects an important theoretical position. Diffusion studies are valuable in their recognition that events external to some social unit have consequences or effects on those units, affecting the probability that similar events will or will not occur. One major concern of Most and Starr (1980) was to highlight the proposition that large-scale conflict events were not independent, and, thus, that there were significant effects on standard research design and the standard use of statistics. O'Loughlin and Witmer (2005, 10), in a review of approaches to the study of civil war, reiterate this point: "Most analyses of social science data have proceeded apace with an implicit assumption that all the data are generated by a random process that results in the data being independently, identically, distributed." Diffusion analyses directly address this core assumption.

Some diffusion approaches also recognize the spatial element of the consequences or effects of events/actions—going beyond simple emulation or prototype-cueing processes—to argue that proximity to some stimuli increases (or decreases) the probability of subsequent behavior or events in nearby social units (see Starr 2003; also Most and Starr 1990). The term "contagion" reflects an epidemiological perspective that sees certain events or stimuli spreading through various forms of contact. Positive spatial diffusion through close proximity (such as contiguity) could be conceptualized as "skin-borne" disease. Regional effects could perhaps be seen as "air-borne" disease—where proximity is still important, but less so than in contiguous situations. It is crucial to distinguish these "contagion" processes from the conceptualization of diffusion simply as emulation, whereby people see some occurrence—no matter how near or far—and change the probabilities of their own behavior through a desire to repeat (or avoid) that occurrence (for example, emulation has been one central focus of those studying the spread of the revolutionary events of the 2010–11 Arab Spring).

The negative view of state failure held by international organizations and state governments rests on perceptions—or assumptions—that there will be a positive spatial contagion of the negative aspects/effects of failure through the spread of the disease to contiguous neighbors or the near region. We are concerned with whether the instability, unrest, civil war, or interstate war, which are connected to state failure/collapse, exhibit such spatial spread. Echoing Most and Starr's analysis (1980) of the diffusion of large-scale social conflict (both internal and external conflict), there are important theoretical reasons why one could hypothesize positive spatial diffusion. As has been argued (for example, Most and Starr 1980; Siverson and Starr 1991), large-scale conflict such as civil war or interstate war, or highly destabilizing situations as state collapse, can significantly affect the opportunities and willingness of nearby areas. Such activities may affect the expected utility of attacking weak nearby targets, or becoming a target oneself from the mobilized armed forces of neighbors (see, for example, Starr 1994). State failure, like civil war, might make states inviting targets for other states; yet any violent or large-scale conflict could promote cascading internal effects in any of the participants—making additional subsequent state failure (or its effects) more likely.

Drawing on the work of Midlarsky (for example, 1975), nearby conflict (or here, state failure) may generate various types of uncertainty and anxiety, and change the probability of certain types of conflictual behavior. Looking at the occurrence of conflict and the possible effects on neighbors, Most and Starr (1980, 935) note that the "important point . . . is that each nation's structure of risks and opportunities is likely to be changed once a war is under way and these changes may be most dramatic for those nations which are proximate to the warring nations."

Here we are making a similar argument about state collapse and its effects on neighbors and neighboring regions. These arguments are also reflected in the following observations by O'Loughlin and Witmer (2005, 3) regarding the influence of geographic context:

> A lack of territorial sovereignty and an inability to form a national identity conspire to keep weak states vulnerable to volatile domestic circumstances. The spatial clustering of weakened states, and the subsequent clustering of conflict in weak states, allows for conflict to cross borders, infecting already vulnerable states. Therefore, the location of a state (and its civil wars) *is not simply an attribute, but another potential cause of conflict* [emphasis added]. States with high risk are subject to increased risk because 1) neighboring wars exacerbate volatile domestic conditions inside border-

ing states, and 2) neighboring wars can (and frequently do) spread into nearby states. Weak states cannot mitigate conflict diffusion and escalation from outside state borders.

While a diffusion approach focuses on external factors and effects, it must always be recognized that the unit of analysis of interest must have some combination of factors that make it "ready for diffusion," thus pulling together both external and internal factors. Here, we hypothesize that negative causal elements for state failure—instability, unrest, civil war, and external war—will diffuse from failed states to nearby states. Given the existing literature demonstrating general diffusion processes at work for both interstate and civil war (see, for example, Most and Starr 1980; Starr and Most 1983, 1985; Siverson and Starr 1991; Gleditsch and Ward 2000; Gleditsch 2002a; Sambanis 2002; or O'Loughlin and Witmer 2005; Salehyan and Gleditsch 2006), we think this is a reasonable hypothesis. The diffusion of these conflict-oriented factors will, in turn, make nearby states "ready" for the diffusion of state failure. Thus, we will address a second hypothesis, that another negative consequence of state failure—failure itself—will also be found to diffuse through spatial contagion.

It should be clear, however, that we are not attempting in this chapter to develop a full model of inter- or intrastate conflict, nor are we attempting to develop a full model of the causes of state failure. The exact conditions that make any state "ready" for "failure" may vary considerably, as the literature noted above indicates (as well as the factors discussed in Chapter Five regarding the repetition of failure). The mechanisms by which failure or its effects spread, are also varied—the diffusion perspective is based on the notion that proximity generates multiple modes of transaction, including flows of people, trade, information, military actions, and so forth. Flows of refugees, ethnic groups that cross borders, the existence of rebel sanctuaries, intergovernmental military cooperation or conflict, economic sanctions or assistance, and the like will all affect opportunity and willingness.[2] With the many variables and possible combinations of variables, there is a degrees of freedom problem—many variables/combinations and only a limited number of state failures. Future work can expand the use of comparative case studies, and help to uncover which mechanisms tend to be at work under different conditions.

DATA AND OPERATIONALIZATION

We argue that in addition to devastation in the state that experiences it, state failure can result in the spread of destabilizing elements at the regional level.

Specifically, we examine the likelihood that the political consequences of state failure would spread to other states; these consequences are political unrest and instability, civil wars, subsequent state failures, and international war. Our empirical analyses, therefore, are designed to evaluate whether—and to what extent—the negative consequences of state collapse diffuse to neighboring and nearby states. We examine regional diffusion of the key consequences of state failure for the period 1950 to 2010, with country-years as the unit of analysis.

DEPENDENT VARIABLES

Given our interest in the destabilizing effects of state failure, we focus on five negative consequences that might spread to other states in the region (see Chapter Three). The first two of these consequences deal with lower levels of political upheaval, and we refer to these as political unrest and instability. These two variables were generated from a principal-components factor analysis of seven different variables indicating domestic political turmoil, obtained from the Banks (2012) dataset. Three of these variables—strikes, riots, and demonstrations—loaded on the first factor, and the other four—revolutions, coups, crises, and guerrilla warfare—loaded more heavily on the second factor. The *Political Unrest* variable is a combined indicator (factor score) for the first factor (strikes, riots, and demonstrations); this is essentially a measure of minor political disturbances. Somewhat more intense aspects of political tumult are indicated by the variable for *Political Instability*, which is the factor score for revolutions, coups, crises, and guerrilla warfare.

The third dependent variable is a dichotomous indicator for the presence of civil war in a given country-year; the *Civil War* variable is coded 1 if there was a civil war and zero in the absence of a civil war. The civil war data were obtained from the UCDP/PRIO Armed Conflict Dataset (Strand et al. 2004).[3] Another violent political consequence of state failure that we assess is international war. The indicator for *International War* is also a dichotomous variable, coded 1 for country-years with an interstate war and zero otherwise. These data were also obtained from the UCDP/PRIO dataset (Strand et al. 2004).[4] The last consequence of state failure we consider is state collapse itself. To assess whether state failure leads to other state failures in nearby states, we include a binary variable for *State Failure* in a given country-year. States with a POLITY IV score of –77 in a given year are considered to have experienced a failure year and are assigned a value of 1 for that year, zero otherwise.

COVARIATES

The main covariates in these analyses include two measures for state failure that account for geography and a separate variable for the overall number of state failures in the system in a given year. The first independent variable is a *Distance-Weighted State Failure* measure that is obtained through the summation of all state failures in the system in a given year, where each one is weighted inversely by the log of the distance from the state in question:

$$\sum_{j=1}^{N_{t-1}} \frac{SF_{ijt}}{\ln(Distance_{ijt})}$$

This continuous variable that measures distance-weighted state failure allows us to assess regional and second-order effects of state collapse. The second independent variable measures the number of state failures that occurred in a given year in contiguous states. The value of the variable for *Collapse in a Contiguous State* ranges from zero to 2. The purpose of including these two geographically adjusted measures of state failure is to discern the relative effects of contiguity and absolute distance on the diffusion of state collapse and its consequences. We expect that the closer a state is to a failed state, the more likely it is to experience the negative effects of state failure discussed above; we expect this relationship to be even stronger for contiguous states. The third covariate deals with the overall level of state failure in the system in a given year and is operationalized as the total number of states that failed in a particular year; the value of *State Failure in the System* ranges from zero to 6. Given that state failure is believed to be regionally destabilizing, intuition might suggest that overall levels of state failure in the system would also have a destabilizing effect. We argue, however, that the diffusion of the effects of state fragility and collapse is a regional dynamic and does not operate at the systemic level. Thus we do not expect the number of failures in the system to have a significant relationship with the dependent variables. Moreover, the inclusion of this variable allows us to control for the effect of the total number of state failures in the system in our analysis of neighborhood and geographical effects.

The control variables in the analysis, drawing on the civil war literature as well as discussions in Chapters Four and Five, include levels of democracy, population, national income, and economic openness. Studies of civil war and political violence suggest that states that are "mixed regimes," neither highly democratic nor extremely autocratic, tend to be unstable and prone to vio-

TABLE 6.1: Summary Statistics

Variables	Mean	Standard deviation	Minimum	Maximum
Dependent Variables				
Unrest (*N*=6596)	0.040	1.065	−4.278	23.584
Instability (*N*=6596)	−0.023	0.937	−5.660	27.109
Civil War (*N*=6690)	0.148	0.355	0	1
International War (*N*=6847)	0.020	0.139	0	1
State Failure (*N*=6768)	0.003	0.057	0	1
Independent Variables				
Distance-Weighted State Failure	0.268	0.120	0	1.297
Collapse in a Contiguous State	0.049	0.217	0	1
State Failures in System	2.201	1.587	0	6
POLITY score	1.077	7.463	−10	10
POLITY score squared	56.857	32.860	0	100
ln(Population)	9.003	1.517	5.251	14.096
ln(GDP)	8.236	1.258	4.764	11.979
ln(Openness)	64.737	45.851	1.035	443.175
Year	1985.62	15.865	1951	2010

lence. To test this proposition with regard to our five dependent variables, we include a variable for regime type, as measured by POLITY IV scores, as well as a squared term for POLITY scores (Marshall and Jaggers 2011). The POLITY scale ranges from −10 (autocracy) to 10 (democracy). We expect a curvilinear relationship between democracy and the dependent variables, with the likelihood of state failure and its negative effects decreasing both at very high and very low levels of democracy. To capture basic socioeconomic effects, we also control for population (measured in millions), national income (GDP per capita/1000), and economic openness (imports and exports as a proportion of national income).[5] The data on population figures and the two economic variables were obtained from the Expanded Trade and GDP Dataset (Gleditsch 2002b). We also include a variable for year to account for the possibility that the dependent variables may be trending in one direction or another over time. Note that all independent variables are lagged one year to account for the effect of time.[6] Summary statistics are presented in Table 6.1.

ANALYSIS AND RESULTS

We employ time-series cross-sectional data in our analyses and, therefore, we estimate a series of random-effects models to assess the likelihood of diffusion of the negative consequences of state failure to neighboring and nearby states. Given that these are panel data, the random-effects models allow us to take into

TABLE 6.2: State Failure and Political Unrest

	Model 1	Model 2
Constant	6.468	6.455
	(2.152)	(2.155)
Distance-Weighted State Failure	−0.008	
	(0.065)	—
Collapse in a Contiguous State		0.073
	—	(0.061)
State Failures in the System		−0.004
	—	(0.008)
POLITY score	0.006**	0.007**
	(0.003)	(0.003)
POLITY score squared	−0.002**	−0.002**
	(0.001)	(0.001)
ln(Population)	0.165**	0.164**
	(0.019)	(0.019)
ln(GDP)	0.079	0.082
	(0.022)	(0.022)
Year	−0.004**	−0.004**
	(0.001)	(0.001)
ln(Openness)	−0.114**	−0.112**
	(0.031)	(0.031)
Year	−0.004**	−0.004**
	(0.001)	(0.001)

Note: NT=6596. Cell entries are random effects coefficient estimates; standard errors are in parentheses. One asterisk indicates $p<0.05$ and two indicate $p<0.01$, one-tailed.

TABLE 6.3: State Failure and Political Instability

	Model 1	Model 2
Constant	12.323	12.806
	(1.970)	(1.974)
Distance-Weighted State Failure	0.072	
	(0.058)	—
Collapse in a Contiguous State		0.094*
	—	(0.055)
State Failures in the System		0.011
	—	(0.007)
POLITY score	−0.003	−0.003
	(0.002)	(0.002)
POLITY score squared	−0.003	−0.003
	(0.00)	(0.00)
ln(Population)	0.035	0.034*
	(0.019)	(0.019)
ln(GDP)	−0.025	−0.021
	(0.021)	(0.021)
ln(Openness)	−0.117**	−0.114**
	(0.029)	(0.029)
Year	−0.006**	−0.006**
	(0.001)	(0.001)

Note: NT=6596. Cell entries are random effects coefficient estimates; standard errors are in parentheses. One asterisk indicates $P<0.05$ and two indicate $p<0.01$, one-tailed.

consideration both the cross-sectional and temporal components of the data.[7] The models assessing the effect of the covariates on the continuous measures for political unrest and instability employ random-effects regression models, and analyses of the effects on the three dichotomous dependent variables (civil war, state failure, and international war) employ random-effects logit models (Hsiao, 2002). For each of our five dependent variables, we estimate two separate models: one that includes the distance-weighted state failure measure, and the other which contains the variable for the number of contiguous states that experienced failure in a given year. Given a high level of correlation between the distance-weighted state failure variable and the variable for overall number of state failures in the system, the latter has been included only in the contiguity models. Below we outline the results of the models for each of our dependent variables.

With respect to the first dependent variable, our findings indicate that collapse in a contiguous state is positively related to unrest, although it is not a statistically significant effect, and this effect does not hold for the distance-weighted measure. We find strong evidence for a curvilinear relationship between democracy and unrest, indicating that states toward the middle of the democracy continuum are the most susceptible to political unrest. The size of the population is positively associated with unrest, and economic openness has a negative effect. Unrest is not significantly affected by the other variables in the model, although there seems to be a negative trend over time. Instability levels are also positively, and significantly, related to state failure in a contiguous state, while the effect of the distance-weighted measure remains insignificant for this variable as well. Failure in a contiguous state increases instability by about one-tenth of a standard deviation. Our expectations for a curvilinear relationship between democracy and instability are not borne out in either model; since the instability measure reflects a somewhat more intense level of political turmoil than the unrest variable, the democracy findings may indicate that mixed regimes are more prone to lower-level protest reactions than either stable democracies or autocratic regimes. The negative effects of both economic openness and the year variable hold in these models as well.

For both indicators of political turmoil (short of war), therefore, our models indicate that *contiguity*—not merely distance—plays a role in the spread of the effects of state collapse, but to a greater extent in the dispersion of instability. This reflects the fact that the diffusion dynamics for these factors are best explained through the consideration of shared state borders. This is consistent with the findings of Iqbal (2007), which suggest that regional flows of refugees are best explained through consideration of contiguity.

TABLE 6.4: State Failure and Civil War

	Model 1	Model 2
Constant	−61.090	−61.518
	(9.700)	(9.703)
Distance-Weighted State Failure	0.412*	
	(0.25)	—
Collapse in a Contiguous State		0.703**
	—	(0.203)
State Failures in the System		0.015
	—	(0.03)
POLITY score	−0.034**	−0.033**
	(0.012)	(0.01)
POLITY score squared	−0.014**	−0.013**
	(0.002)	(0.002)
ln(Population)	0.612**	0.605**
	(0.145)	(0.145)
ln(GDP)	−0.163	−0.134
	(0.127)	(0.128)
ln(Openness)	−0.648**	−0.617**
	(0.131)	(0.132)
Year	0.028**	0.029**
	(0.005)	(0.005)

Note: NT=6690. Cell entries are random effects logit estimates; standard errors are in parentheses. One asterisk indicates $P<0.05$ and two indicate $P<0.01$, one-tailed.

Both models evaluating the effect of the covariates on the incidence of civil war suggest that state failure increases the likelihood of civil war in nearby and neighboring states. The coefficients for both the distance-weighted state failure variable as well as the variable for collapse in a contiguous state are positive and significant, although the latter displays a higher level of significance. This suggests that civil war is a consequence of state failure that diffuses to contiguous states, as well as states that are close by. This implies the presence of salient diffusion processes for one of the most destabilizing factors associated with state failure: civil war. And the dispersion of this effect does not require a shared border. With respect to the control variables, the size of the population is also positively associated with civil war, although the curvilinear effect of democracy is less obvious than in the models assessing unrest and instability. Democracy does, however, appear to have a direct negative effect on the incidence of civil war. And we again see a negative influence of economic openness, but—unlike the models for unrest and instability—the year variable displays a positive effect on civil war. That is not surprising, since the global system has indeed witnessed an increase in the number of civil wars since the end of the Cold War.

TABLE 6.5: State Failure and International War

	Model 1	Model 2
Constant	60.169	61.305
	(16.848)	(16.953)
Distance-Weighted State Failure	−0.363	
	(0.584)	—
Collapse in a Contiguous State		−0.934
	—	(0.517)
State Failures in the System		−0.014
	—	(0.074)
POLITY score	−0.025	−0.027
	(0.024)	(0.024)
POLITY score squared	−0.005	−0.005
	(0.004)	(0.004)
ln(Population)	0.671**	0.673**
	(0.146)	(0.146)
ln(GDP)	−0.232	−0.252
	(0.171)	(0.172)
ln(Openness)	0.275	0.240
	(0.206)	(0.207)
Year	−0.036**	−0.036**
	(0.009)	(0.009)

Note: NT=6847. Cell entries are random effects logit estimates; standard errors are in parentheses. One asterisk indicates $P<0.05$ and two indicate $P<0.01$, one-tailed.

TABLE 6.6: State Failure and State Failure

	Model 1	Model 2
Constant	−36.57	−39.513
	(32.73)	(32.68)
Distance-Weighted State Failure	−0.193	
	(1.11)	—
Collapse in a Contiguous State		−0.996
	—	(1.057)
State Failures in the System		−0.002
	—	(0.145)
POLITY score	0.048	0.047
	(0.04)	(0.04)
POLITY score squared	−0.015*	−0.016*
	(0.009)	(0.009)
ln(Population)	−0.401**	−0.395**
	(0.166)	(0.165)
ln(GDP)	−0.705**	−0.725**
	(0.25)	(0.25)
ln(Openness)	−0.711*	−0.734*
	(0.33)	(0.33)
Year	0.022	0.023
	(0.017)	(0.017)

Note: NT=6768. Cell entries are random effects logit estimates; standard errors are in parentheses. One asterisk indicates $P<0.05$ and two indicate $P<0.01$, one-tailed.

The findings of an earlier work (Iqbal and Starr 2008) revealed a significantly positive effect of both the distance-weighted state failure measure and the indicator for collapse in contiguous states on the incidence of international war. However, the current analysis does not find support for the hypothesis that state failure creates possible incentives for violent behavior with other states, and that the failed state itself may present an especially attractive target for invasion, thus providing opportunities for interstate armed conflict. These models do not provide evidence that state failure results in an increase in the incidence of international war. In the previous analysis (Iqbal and Starr 2008), which focused on the time period of 1946 to 1999, we found that state failure was, in fact, positively associated with higher occurrence of international conflict. With the addition of eleven post–Cold War years, the association with interstate war dissipates. This is not tremendously surprising, since the international system after the Cold War has experienced a steady decline in all sorts of international war. There is clear empirical evidence that the primary type of armed conflict since the end of the Cold War has been intrastate. The systemic climate during the Cold War had the dual effect of cultivating hostilities among countries and, at the same time, exercising certain controls that stabilized domestic political regimes. The superpowers—in both blocs—lent support to governments that, once the Cold War dynamics had ceased, were no longer able to maintain control. As a result, the post–Cold War period has seen an increase in state failures and very few international wars. The incidence was, on average, twice as high during the period 1991 to 2010 as it was from 1946 to 1990.

As in the previous models in this study, population is positively related to interstate conflict, and there is a minor negative effect of wealth. The models indicate a negative trend in international conflict over time, which reflects a historical decrease in interstate wars over the decades, particularly in the post–Cold War era. Note that there is no evidence of a curvilinear relationship between democracy and interstate conflict, which is consistent with the arguments in the democratic peace literature (see, for example, Russett 1993; Ray 1998).

Although our analysis reveals that states geographically close to a failed state (and especially for contiguous states) are likely to experience a civil war, that effect does not hold for state failure itself. Interestingly, neither of our models indicates that state failure is spatially contagious. The models assessing state failure as the dependent variable show a significantly negative influence of GDP, however, which is different from the effect (rather lack thereof) for the other dependent variables but consistent with our expectations. Importantly, the somewhat counterintuitive finding about the lack of contagion effects in state failure reflects the fact that state collapse is *distinct* from other phenomena of political violence with which it is often associated, such as civil war. Our findings suggest that the regional threats posed by failing states are associated with instances of domestic and international violence of various magnitudes, but not a domino effect with respect to state collapse itself. State failure results from unique combinations of the characteristics of individual states, and, therefore, certain domestic conditions may cause some states to fail while others remain alive (that is, make them "ready" for the diffusion of state failure). This is an internal, or domestic, argument. There is an external, or international, argument as well. As discussed in Chapter Five, given a state failure in some country, a set of IGOs along with one or more major powers (and a number of regional powers) will often mobilize to provide political and material support to the failed state and those nearby—especially given the perception and reality that various negative consequences of state failure will spread.

It should be noted that none of the dependent variables are affected by the overall number of state failures in the system. This finding is consistent with our argument that state failure negatively affects other states within close proximity and, as a result, can contribute to regional instability. The highest number of state failures in a given year is six, and it stands to reason that unless at least one of those failures is in a nearby or neighboring state, the likelihood of political violence does not increase. This emphasizes the importance of location, geography, and spatial dispersion in the understanding of issues related to domestic and international violence. If the diffusion of the consequences of state failure were a systemwide phenomenon (with a strong basis in some form of emulation), then these effects—such as civil wars—would rise as the number of failures increase. In that case, the variable for the total number of failures would capture that relationship and the distance-related measures would not add significantly to the explanatory power of the model. The results of our analyses, however, reveal the opposite pattern; the effects of variables for both distance-weighted state failure and failure in a contiguous state on the phenomena of interest are significant, whereas the global measure has no significant effect.

Taken together, the findings of our analyses imply that the consequences of state failure in terms of political violence do, in fact, geographically disperse and, therefore, may be destabilizing at the regional level. The consequences of state collapse that fall short of actual war (unrest and instability) spread only to contiguous states. Of particular note, however, is evidence that the diffusion of civil war is explained by both contiguity and distance. That is, these consequences are likely to spread to nearby states even in the absence of a shared border. Contiguous states, however, are the most vulnerable to this diffusion effect.

CONCLUSION

Our analyses indicate several major points regarding the regional effects of state failure. First, there are indeed spatial effects associated with collapsed states. Such states, which are generated by political instability and armed conflict, in turn generate subsequent unrest, instability, and interstate and civil war in their neighbors and near regions. Our analyses seem to indicate that the more "minor" possible consequences of state failure—political unrest and instability—spread to a lesser degree than more intense forms of violence—civil and interstate war. Following Most and Starr (1989), a quick review of some "stylized facts" indicates that this finding has face validity. Looking at all ninety-eight of the country-years in which a state failure occurred (according to our measure of –77 on the POLITY scale), there is a new or ongoing civil war in 60 percent of those years.[8]

Second, state failure itself is not contagious, although some if its major consequences are. This finding reinforces our discussion concerning the conceptualization of state failure in that state failure conceptualized as collapse is clearly not the same as civil war, and that civil war by itself cannot be a simple proxy for state failure. Given that this most extreme consequence of failure does not appear to diffuse either to contiguous neighbors, the regional neighborhood, or in the international system, we are led to ask: what happens internally or externally that shields neighbors from this form of diffusion? As noted below, this is a key finding that raises a number of directions for future research.

Third, instability and political unrest appear to spread through contiguity, but not through a distance-weighted measure of state failure. On the other hand, the diffusion of civil war is reflected in both measures of proximity. Hence, our findings support the position that distance-weighted measures and geographic contiguity tap two related, but not identical, dimensions of proximity and its effects. And, as noted, diffusion thus appears to be regional as well as affecting first-order neighbors. This conclusion is further strengthened by the lack of a significant effect of the global measure for state failure on the phenomena of political violence under consideration. Although state failure in a nearby or neighboring state significantly increases armed conflict and other aspects of domestic political upheaval, the total number of states collapsing in the system in a given year has no effect.

Our findings add to a growing literature on the diffusion of violent conflict. One of the future projects to which this research points is a fuller examination of the diffusion of interstate conflict and of civil war, including the various ways the two forms of major conflict are related to each other. We have found civil war to be a major factor in the collapse of states. In turn, the current analyses indicate that civil war does diffuse to the neighbors/region of collapsed states.

There are also a number of future directions for research specifically directed at state failure. As noted above, the exact mechanisms by which the conflict-oriented diffusion effects generated by failing states take place need to be investigated. Comparative case studies will also be needed for this purpose, which was not directly addressed in Chapter Five. The present analysis has, indeed, paid most attention to the political/military consequences of collapse. There are, however, also a variety of nonpolitical consequences, including economic, social, and human security consequences of state collapse and violent conflict (see, for example, Iqbal 2006). The investigation of economic and social consequences must take into account the finding here that democracy has a strong curvilinear effect on state collapse—with collapse least likely at both the highest and lowest levels of democracy: an effect that was noted in Chapter Five.

Ultimately, we need to return to the policy concerns that were raised in the introductory chapter. The growing research agenda on various aspects of state failure must be aimed at devising policy prescriptions for managing and preventing the negative domestic and regional effects of state failure, as well as for preventing future failures. More broadly, such research will be instrumental in identifying effective ways for states and international organizations to address issues of instability, internal conflict, and development—especially during the highly vulnerable period of transition to democracy.

Our research has raised a critical question: why doesn't state failure itself diffuse? This question relates directly to the various forms of early warning and intervention systems generated by international organizations and state governments. Scholars must look more closely at how IGOs (such as the United Nations and its various organizations, the World Bank, the IMF, or regional actors such as the EU or ECOWAS) and states move to identify and deal with "at risk" states. We propose here that many such "at risk" or fragile states have been affected by the diffusion of the negative effects of state failure. Timely interventions might be an important factor in the lack of diffusion of state failure. Further study of what makes such interventions effective would be another focus of future research. And, intervention by whom? As we will see in the next chapter, for economic and security support some argue that the United Nations and other multilateral institutions, or the major powers, should take the lead (for example, Mueller 2004). Some findings on the democratic peace seem to indicate that stable and developed democracies might be crucial in helping "endangered" democracies avoid failure (for example, Simon and Starr 2000). In other areas, the lead may have been taken by NGOs. One thing is clear: the present analyses have raised a number of questions, and that much work remains to find the answers.

7 State Failure: Prevention and Management

INTRODUCTION

In this penultimate chapter, we discuss the policy implications of our analyses, both in terms of preventing state failure and as they relate to the management and recovery of collapsed states. As we have said, in general, much of the analysis of state failure can be seen as an exercise in policy evaluation. Previous investigators and commentators have uniformly considered state failure a dangerous phenomenon, with dire consequences at both the local and regional levels. Working from this belief, policy prescriptions have focused on forestalling such negative consequences. It should also be repeated that in the move to policy, we must take into account the different definitions of "failure." It is here that the various conceptualizations of failure that focus on state weakness, instability, or fragility become more relevant.

Still, before we can have much confidence in any policy prescriptions, a number of analytic tasks, such as those outlined above, must be undertaken. Our findings can be used to help survey the set of policy recommendations extant in the scholarly and policy literatures, and in selecting the most promising avenues of policy choice and implementation, especially in forestalling recurrence or mitigating diffusion effects, and in directing our attention to those states with the greatest hazard of collapse. With these analyses in hand, we can evaluate past policy choices and provide future policy prescriptions for both states and international organizations. Our findings, especially from Chapters Five and Six, have clear implications for policy issues related to political and economic development in terms of international organization intervention, foreign aid, development, and democracy.

The various ways in which analysts and policy-makers have addressed policy related to state failure generally translate into two basic areas:

(1) Intervention
(2) Recovery

Much of the work on "intervention" deals with the role and impact of inter-governmental organizations, including regional organizations but most especially the activity of the United Nations and its various organs and agencies. Of interest are a number of proposals for changing the role of the UN, and how its role might evolve. Policy on intervention also concerns aid in its various forms, both multilateral and bilateral, as introduced in the case studies presented in Chapter Five.

The work on "recovery" involves both the evaluation of various forms of intervention and the measurement of recovery: turnarounds from some condition of "failure"/weakness/instability; moving away from some threshold of weakness/instability/fragility; general notions of improvement across any number of indicators of economic, political, or social development. In their focus on postconflict reconstruction, Hamre and Sullivan (2002) argue that "recovery" is a term preferable to "nation-building."[1]

Approaches to both intervention and recovery have a commonality in that almost all such analysis or policy prescription is ultimately directed toward a third basic area: (3) Prevention and/or early warning. Thus while there is a two-headed arrow between (1) and (2), there is also a separate arrow from each to (3).

INTERVENTION: FOREIGN AID

If we return to the survey of different conceptualizations and definitions of state failure, all of them reflect in some way or another one or more dimensions in which the state or states in question *lack* some resource, capacity, or quality: they are weak, or poor, or fragile, or unstable, or do not possess economic and/or political development, or strong institutions to manage conflict (violent or nonviolent political conflict/contestation). We may perhaps summarize this problem using Carment et al.'s formulation (2006) of the "authority, legitimacy, and capacity" triangle. Failed states lack capacity (economic, political/legal, social) to maintain institutions and governance (see also Carment et al. 2008; and Sobek 2010).

It is not surprising, therefore, that often an initial policy approach to state failure takes the form of bilateral or dyadic policies by which one state attempts to provide assistance and resources to create or increase the capacity of a state perceived to be failing or in danger of failing, or to turn around a state already deemed to have failed. Even if donor states also contribute to multilateral aid through IGOs (and the types of aid provided by IGOs may take different forms from bilateral aid), state-to-state foreign aid is quite often the first type of "intervention" activity that is undertaken. It should be clear that a concern with aid involves conceptions of failure in terms of economics and development. Indeed, Chauvet and Collier (2008) are explicit in characterizing their work as using an economic definition of a failing state, based on the Country Policy and Institutional Assessment (CPIA) measure developed by the World Bank. Here a country is seen as "failed" by scoring 2.5 or less on the CPIA for four successive years. A turnaround from failure is indicated by four successive years of a CPIA score of 3.5 or more.

We have already noted in Chapter Five that certain types of foreign aid, or official development assistance (ODA), especially as provided to nondemocratic governments, may not have any effect on alleviating resource or capacity problems, and indeed may generate unanticipated and highly negative effects on the conditions of authority, legitimacy, or state capacity. A good deal of research flowing from the political survival model of Bueno de Mesquita and colleagues (and related research, such as that of Girod 2012) indicate that "free goods" or "windfall income" or what Chauvet and Collier (2008) call "natural resource rents" will only promote corruption and kleptocracy, and be used to support the ability of small selectorates and small winning coalitions to keep autocrats in power. This research also demonstrates how such "free goods" can also have detrimental effects on the provision of broadly distributed collective goods to the state's population (see also Ades and Di Tella 1999).[2] From the viewpoint of Carment et al. (2008), this means that most aid will do little to prevent state failure, or from Chauvet and Collier's viewpoint (2008), will have no impact on the ability of a failed state to generate a sustained turnaround. Bueno de Mesquita and Smith (2009b, 196) are quite blunt about foreign aid: "At best, foreign aid is an inefficient means through which to improve welfare in developing countries. At worst, foreign aid induces a decline in economic activity and social welfare and retards democratization. Although foreign aid provides leaders with the resources to promote social welfare, it provides them with the political incentive to do just the opposite."

In terms of policy, Bueno de Mesquita and Smith (2007) conclude:

> Our model offers important policy advice for those who wish to help the needy around the world. Receiving aid is most likely to improve the welfare of citizens in large coalition systems. In such systems, the majority of the additional resources are

allocated to public goods, and the leader can retain only limited resources for her own discretionary projects. Aid given to such systems is likely to promote economic growth and enhance social welfare. U.S. reconstruction aid to Western Europe under the Marshall Plan is an example of such a success story. (pp. 280–81)

Thus, just as Chauvet and Collier (2008) and Carment et al. (2008) argue that technical aid will have a greater positive impact, Smith (2008, 791) notes that "aid programs designed to enhance standard public goods provisions, such as vaccinations and other public health programs, are more likely to be successful than programs that promote freedom of information, government transparency, or coordination skills." Bueno de Mesquita and Smith (2009b) explicitly note that if democratization is part of the goal (as we see in many policy discussions about state failure), programs such as the Millennium Challenge grants are unlikely to help, and more likely to work against the goal of democratization. Carment et al. (2006; 2008) argue that donors must think closely about types of aid, and how to work in the development of legitimacy—as is clearly done with the selectorate model. Returning to discussions found in Chapter Five, much of the advice about foreign aid, and critiques of foreign aid programs, return to the issue of legitimacy and of political reform taking temporal and policy precedence to generate economic reform. Bueno de Mesquita and Smith (2007, 281) specifically note: "In terms of promoting development, the theory's implications are clear: political reform needs to precede economic development."

While much more broadly applicable to a variety of policy approaches to state failure, the observations of Eizenstat et al. (2005, 138–39) are relevant here. They note four lessons to be learned from previous attempts to "stabilize" (that is to aid and develop) weak or failed states. The first is most important here: "[M]oney cannot buy effective governance." But as we also saw in Chapter Five, the second lesson is also key: donors and donor programs must deal with local elites. The third and fourth lessons apply to the policy time frame: short-term actions must not be allowed to make the situation/problems worse; and all parties involved must recognize the long-term nature of the situation/policy.

INTERVENTION: POLICING INTERNAL CONFLICTS

Part of the policy debate, and one point noted above, is that some level of internal stability, legitimacy of governance, and the attendant conditions of institutional resilience and effectiveness should probably precede attempts for major economic reforms and the injection of resources. One major dimension in the factors causing state failure across a number of models is conflict—particularly lethal violent conflict, and particularly the more extreme forms of insurrection and civil war (with civil war exhibiting the strongest diffusion effects, as shown in Chapter Six). In dealing with policy, we highlight the importance of several issues raised in Chapter Two, especially understanding the different definitions of failure and the different approaches to failure. By focusing on internal conflict there is at least an implicit argument that some form of "stabilization" of a situation must occur, and that it must take precedence over other activities. "Stabilization" is a focus of Blair and Fitz-Gerald (2009). Citing the United Kingdom's Government Stabilisation Unit's definition, stabilization "is a summary term for the complex processes that have to be undertaken in countries experiencing, or emerging from, violent conflict to achieve peace and security and a political settlement that leads to legitimate government" (2009, 4). They also add material from British doctrine found in JDP 3–40, *Security and Stabilisation: The Military Contribution*, which specifies that stabilization is "the process that supports states which are entering, enduring or emerging from conflict, in order to prevent or reduce violence; protect the population and key infrastructure; promote political processes and governance structures" (2009, 4).

This view of what first needs to be done fits well with John Mueller's proposals to "police the remnants of war" (2003, 2004). Mueller sees the greatest portion of contemporary violence as internal, but with the following characteristics that make it amenable to external intervention:

> Moreover, much, but not all, of what remains of war is substantially opportunistic predation waged by packs of criminals, bandits, and thugs who engage in warfare in much the same way as they often did in medieval and early modern Europe: as mercenaries recruited or dragooned by weak (or even desperate) state governments or as warlord gangs developed within failed or weak states. Much of this warfare could be reduced or substantially eliminated by disciplined police and military forces and, in their new era of essential consensus in the wake of the Cold War, the developed countries could create mechanisms for policing civil warfare . . . . The key lies in the establishment of competent domestic military and policing forces. (2003, 507)

Mueller sees this approach as reflecting the Canadian policy of POGG—peace, order, and good government. By "policing the remnants of war," a good deal of stabilization could be achieved in a number of countries or regions. This view is also consistent with the analysis of Hamre and Sullivan (2002, 90), who note: "The goal, during the short-to-medium run, is to create a minimally capable state, not to build a nation or address all the root causes that imperil peace. Those goals involve a longer-term process that is beyond the scope of what external actors can achieve or lead; actors within the country itself must do so." Looking at the eight cases discussed in Chapter Five, we can see where this approach has worked—and where it has been ineffective. Perhaps the best example of where some form of POGG has worked was the Solomon Islands, which probably had the best combination of factors to avoid a second collapse. The regional peacekeeping operation that began in 2003 (RAMSI) through the fifteen states of the Pacific Islands Forum, including Australia and New Zealand, appears to have worked in the Solomon Islands along the lines argued by Mueller. The ECOWAS intervention in Guinea-Bissau also had positive effects. These two cases might be seen as employing Hamre and Sullivan's "neighborhood watch" system policy (2002), which relies on using regional IGOs.

We do have two examples of what might be considered failures of a POGG approach, in Afghanistan and in the DRC. These cases seem to underscore that Mueller's policy recommendations really must be used in situations that truly involve "remnants" of internal war, and not major secessionist civil wars (or dealing with superpowers as parties to the conflict).

Recall as well that Mueller stresses the need for the use of local/domestic personnel—police and military forces—*supplemented* by external aid. Going back to our discussion of legitimacy in Chapter Five, the local component appears to be crucial for the ultimate success of any such policing interventions. Given Mueller's analogy to the kings of medieval Europe who relied on mercenaries, and his connection between weak governments and the rise of criminal activity, a possibly useful policy area to draw from would be the effects of such "policing" interventions in the case of contemporary maritime piracy (see Daxecker and Prins 2011). One result of their analysis is that, even with considerable European Union and American activity, piracy continues in certain areas. Without local assistance, even the more modest recommendations of Mueller may be ineffective. As Daxecker and Prins (2011, 7) note: "[In] countries with weak or failing governments, local police forces and bureaucratic officials may be more likely to facilitate piracy rather than hinder it so as to share in the proceeds from the sale of plundered goods or ransom rewards." Thus external intervention, while useful, is not enough even in this much narrower area of conflict.[3] Their overall findings regarding high seas piracy also return to themes found in Chapter Five regarding institutional weakness:

> Yet our findings also indicate that some factors are more relevant in predicting piracy

than others, documenting that institutional weakness has the largest effect on mod-els' predictive power for all types of piracy incidents. It thus appears that improving governance mechanisms would carry the most promise in reducing the incidence of piracy and should be more effective than focusing on economic opportunities, improvements in military capacity, or the policing of coastlines.(Daxecker and Prins 2011, 23)[4]

The focus of Mueller, and related approaches to state failure, is directly on the quality of governmental policies. One example is his discussion of counter-productive brutal over-reactions of governments to opposition parties/groups or protests of government policy. Such over-reactions, as discussed in the anti–guerrilla war literature of the 1960s and 1970s, serve only to radicalize and mo-bilize populations. The conclusion to draw from Mueller's analysis is that it is *not* poverty or lack of economic development, but bad governmental policies. Let us note an important boundary-crossing moment here—between basic re-search and policy recommendations. At various points in our analyses we have drawn from the selectorate theory of political survival developed by Bueno de Mesquita and colleagues. Applications of this model demonstrate how the logic of political survival, especially in small selectorate and winning coalition coun-tries, continually leads to bad policies. It also highlights the policy difficulties of including local actors and authorities while achieving "good" policy.

Mueller helps to summarize this discussion, as well as reprising one of the conclusions at the end of Chapter Five, drawing on Blair and Fitz-Gerald (2009), regarding the importance of the rule of law in stabilization and legiti-macy:

> Thus, the establishment of effective government or, more specifically, of coherent and responsive political systems and disciplined military and policing forces, is the key to engendering and maintaining civil peace—to policing the thugs, brigands, bandits, highwaymen, goons, bullies, criminals, pirates, mercenaries, robbers, adven-turers, hooligans, and children who seem to be the chief remaining perpetrators of a type of violence that can be said to resemble war. (Mueller 2003, 513)

Below, in discussing possible roles and strategies for the United Nations, we will return to Mueller's policing concept in regard to "peace maintenance" as an alternative to the standard view of UN peace-keeping strategies.

INTERVENTION: THE ROLE OF THE UNITED NATIONS

The issue of "policing by developed countries," as proposed by Mueller, raises many issues discussed by analysts and policy-makers in regard to the nature, form, and degree of UN intervention to prevent state failure, to ameliorate state failure, and/or to reverse state failure. These issues involve the specter of neocolonialism, the return of imperial powers and a hierarchical imperial system, and a broader discussion of UN encroachment on state sovereignty—all of which finds strong opposition among LDC's, former colonial territories, nondemocratic autocracies, as well as policy-makers and analysts for whom the Westphalian legal concept of "sovereignty" remains an important cornerstone of the state system. Such opposition could, in part, explain the argument that in order to be effective, IGO interventions need to be partnered with local domestic personnel and political authority—but with external aid. Mueller (2003) makes such an argument, as does Kaplan (2010, 89) in discussing what he calls the "unimaginative" international policy in Somalia. He argues that a key problem was that the policy ignored the local sociopolitical context, as compared with what he sees as the successes in Somaliland, where local elites, local customs, and the like were part of policy development and execution.[5] However, other observers (Langford cites Richardson 1996; and Herbst 1996–97) see an unavoidable tension between the right of self-determination and notion of Westphalian sovereignty. They argue that it might be time to find another organizing principle for the international system; one way, suggested Richardson, would be to recognize multiple sovereignties.

Langford (1999, 59) summarizes in part the policy debate: "One camp suggests the engagement of comprehensive state-building mechanisms by resurrecting trusteeship-like arrangements, while others argue for something less. Critical opposition to these proposals claim the immorality, illegality, and infeasibility of such measures." A number of critics wish to return to some form of a UN trusteeship system (as will be discussed below) because of the ineffectiveness of current and past intervention strategies.

While the end of the Cold War brought about a whole range of "peacekeeping" activities that have gone far beyond Cold War–era missions that would simply keep warring parties apart (see, for example, Diehl 2008),[6] many have argued that these "something less" activities have been inadequate. Our case studies from Chapter Five are inconclusive here. While we found that in some cases intervention by regional IGOs or the United Nations did not prevent a first collapse (or even a second), we did see that the matched cases that avoided a second collapse did tend to have a better managed intervention with more resources, and greater use of combined local-international (regional IGO or UN) personnel and resources. An example often used in the policy literature on UN response to state failure is the case of Cambodia summarized briefly in Chapter Five.[7] The "success" in Cambodia has led some (for example, Chopra 1996, 1998) to discuss "peace maintenance" as an alternative to peacekeeping or peace enforcement. This looks much like POGG, and calls for a "unifying concept" or strategy, including diplomatic, military, and humanitarian activities (Langford 1999, 76).

One critic of the "something less" approach has been Stephen Krasner (for example, 2004). He notes the reluctance of many to challenge or move away from traditional notions of sovereignty, and as such, they have relied on a number of "transitional administration" models—that do not challenge sovereignty—by which to bring UN presence to state failure situations. He argues that the demands on such transitional mechanisms are high, and rarely matched by adequate resources (as hinted at in some of the peacekeeping missions noted in Chapter Five; regarding the United Nations in the first DRC collapse and ECOWAS in the Ivory Coast). The use of these mechanisms also becomes difficult in situations in which the various parties to the local political conflicts strongly disagree about both ends and means. Krasner also notes that stability is rarely achieved because of the temporary nature of the transitional administration created through the UN. Krasner summarizes his position thus:

> The current menu of policy instruments for dealing with collapsed and failing states is paltry, consisting primarily of transitional administration and foreign assistance to improve governance, both of which assume that in more or less short order, targeted states can function effectively on their own. Nation building or state-building efforts are almost always described in terms of empowering local authorities to assume the responsibilities of conventional sovereignty. The role of external actors is understood to be limited with regard to time, if not scope, in the case of transitional administration exercising full executive authority. (Krasner 2004, 86)

Krasner's response is to add to the menu of policy options. He presents two new institutional options: (1) return to some idea of trusteeship or protectorate ("probably de facto rather than de jure"); and (2) some version of shared sovereignty. Similarly, regarding (1), Helman and Ratner (1992–93) had earlier proposed that it was time for the United Nations to consider a form of "conservatorship." They note that the mandate system of the League of Nations and the UN's trusteeship system were not applied to independent states, and have used a variety of ("something less") mechanisms that would not appear to violate state sovereignty. They see their view of conservatorship as going much beyond the Cambodia model. They draw an analogy to domestic law, and end with an argument that traditional views of sovereignty will not work in instances of state failure (or collapse):

> The conceptual basis for the effort should lie in the idea of conservatorship. In domestic systems when the polity confronts persons who are utterly incapable of functioning on their own, the law often provides some regime whereby the community itself manages the affairs of the victim. Forms of guardianship or trusteeship are a common response to broken families, serious mental or physical illness, or economic destitution. The hapless individual is placed under the responsibility of a trustee or guardian, who is charged to look out for the best interests of that person .... It is time that the United Nations consider such a response to the plight of failed states .... The traditional view of sovereignty has so decayed that all should recognize the appropriateness of U.N. measures inside member states to save them from self-destruction. (Helman and Ratner 1992–93, 12)

Langford (1999, 66) has identified such writers as Ali Mazrui, William Pfaff, and Paul Johnson, along with Helman and Ratner, as a group who argue "that the UN must recognize the inadequacies of its current methods and utilize past trusteeship experience to build a more comprehensive approach to failed or failing states .... This is achieved through massive intervention by an external actor or group of actors seeking to aid in restoring the capability of self-government." Advocates of this approach recognize that this is no easy task, and any implementation faces a range of difficulties (see, for example, Helman and Ratner 1992–93, 18–19; Langford 1999, 68; Krasner 2004, 106–7). This list always starts with dealing with the power of sovereignty as an idea, as well as "colonial guilt." Another major problem noted by Langford (1999, 70) is this: "The central purpose of proposing a trusteeship system is to help create sustainable governments, but local interests are undermined if the government set up by the trustee does not reflect the indigenous population." We have some evidence to support this view from the case studies in Chapter Five. The range of difficulties is daunting: from deciding when a state has failed, to deciding/assigning the authority to oversee the trusteeship or conservatorship, to determining duration/assessment/termination, to the incredibly thorny question of who bears the financial burdens (especially if the trusteeship itself is a failure), to the writing of treaties, assignment or reassignment of sovereignty, and so forth.

This neatly brings us back to Krasner's second possible policy option: shared sovereignty. Drawing on past shared-sovereignty agreements, both political and economic (as well as the use of international "condominiums" and protectorates), Krasner notes that such arrangements could be created through various forms of agreements such as treaties or contracts. The use of voluntary agreements would also avoid the issue of removing sovereignty as the central organizing principle for the international system:

> Shared sovereignty would involve the engagement of external actors in some of the domestic authority structures of the target state for an indefinite period of time. Such arrangements would be legitimated by agreements signed by recognized national authorities. National actors would use their international legal sovereignty to enter into agreements that would compromise their Westphalian/Vatellian sovereignty with the goal of improving domestic sovereignty. One core element of sovereignty—voluntary agreements—would be preserved, while another core element—the principle of autonomy—would be violated . . . . For policy purposes, it would be best to refer to shared sovereignty as "partnerships." (Krasner 2004, 108)

INTERVENTION: SOME CONCLUDING REMARKS

In Chapter Three, we found a set of predictors for state failure, including both internal conflict—from internal unrest (including strikes, riots, and demonstrations) to full-fledged civil war—and external, or state-to-state war or intervention. In Chapter Six we demonstrated that the same phenomena that help cause collapse may also diffuse after a state collapse. Some phenomena will diffuse to contiguous neighbors, and others to both contiguous neighbors and to the surrounding region.

In Chapter Three, we also found that civil war had the greatest causal impact. While external war was also important, it was less so, and had about the same impact as internal instability. It would seem that for these less intense forms of internal conflict, POGG and related UN peacekeeping types of activities could be effective strategies in possibly preventing collapse in states, a recurrence of collapse, or the diffusion of collapse.[8] Preliminary results from the Chapter Five case studies (about reinforcement rather than positive spatial diffusion) also provide support for this conclusion. However, for more intense and violent civil war (especially internationalized cases), a POGG strategy appears to be a less effective policy choice. It also seems inappropriate for external war, where a sufficiently large peacekeeping/peace-enforcing intervention of the more traditional kind would be needed.

In regard to recovery or "turnaround," several streams of research appear to converge on the types of foreign aid or ODA that would be most effective, and more particularly those forms that would have the least impact, no impact, or even deleterious impact. In regard to the economic dimension, we are thrown back to the post–World War II and postcolonial puzzle of economic development, and it would be presumptuous for us to claim a policy solution for it. However, in cases of massive or total economic collapse extraordinary effort appears to be required. In that case it seems that some form of trustee-ship (or Krasner's "protectorate" or Helman and Ratner's "conservatorship") requires close consideration, including all of the major difficulties briefly out-lined above.

The political, institutional, and legal components needed for recovery would seem to require important local participation, leadership, and input, based around the issues of legitimacy raised in Chapter Five. In addition, recall the analysis of "frailty" in Chapter Three, which highlighted the importance of state-specific factors. The analyses in both Chapters Three and Five point to one important conclusion: that in forming policy we should be careful to avoid looking for, or imposing, "one-size-fits-all" solutions. Helman and Rat-ner (1992–93), for example, note that different solutions are needed for "weak states," states that have already failed, and for failed states where no authority exists (the lattermost seemingly the closest to our use of "collapse" in this proj-ect). It is in the last category, for example, that they suggest the use of a trustee-ship strategy. Similarly, Langford (1999, 76) cites the work of Chopra and his idea of a "UN Directorate" with "four transitional scenarios": (1) a *governorship* for full collapse, where the directorate assumes full control of the government; (2) *control,* in which the directorate exercises powers of "direct control" over all aspects of state authority and rule of law; (3) *partnership,* with the directorate partnering with local authority, but retaining the final policy-making author-ity; and (4) *assistance,* where "the directorate provides an overall coherence and international standard for the development of government structures, selec-tively correcting flaws in the local system." A combination of partnership and assistance can be found in the Cambodian case.

Overall, the work presented here on the analysis of *recurrence* appears to be highly relevant to issues of *recovery.* Recall that the matched cases discussed in Chapter Five had indeed suffered one failure, in terms of collapse. Some very suggestive patterns were uncovered in comparing their postcollapse situations with their matched cases, which also had a second collapse.

EARLY WARNING AND PREVENTION

Hamre and Sullivan (2002) have argued that the international community cannot wait until states fail but must be proactive beforehand. They are not alone on this matter. For example, Hales and Miller (2010, 1) introduce a report contracted to the Canadian Department of National Defense thusly:

> The Adversarial Intent Section (AIS) of Defence Research and Development Canada Toronto has embarked on a project to explore developing a predictive early warning model. The implicit understanding is that improvement in forecasting state failure is linked to an identification of underlying causal factors and increased statistical validity. A predictive early warning model could be used to inform foreign policy formulation, shape preventive/pre-emptive intervention and consequence mitigation.

While their starting point was the Political Instability Task Force (PITF), because of known weaknesses of this model (or any single model), they also looked at and evaluated eight other models.[9] One of the more striking observations when looking across these models is the sense of convergence—although each model varies in terms of schema and indicators, all incorporate political, economic, and social perspectives (and many are based on the same source data, POLITY IV).

We can expand on one clear distinction seen between an applied policy approach, such as early warning systems that would prompt action on the part of outside international actors, and the sort of basic research that we present in Chapters Three to Six (but particularly in Chapters Three and Four). In the basic research we drew from the literature and engaged in analyses that would identify broad causal factors for state collapse. In studies that focus on early warning systems, the focus had shifted from such causal factors to the "triggers" that could act as catalytic agents that can bring together the causal factors and create a reaction that results in collapse.

Indeed, "triggers" are a major focus of Hales and Miller (2010). They note underlying causes, and the generation of data that permit the measure of development, as two main elements needed in the creation of risk assessments. But they go on to highlight "tripwires" or "triggering events," which they see as "underappreciated" (2010, 1–2). Their argument is that understanding and identifying underlying factors are insufficient by themselves. These factors produce some combination of conditions that will lead to state failure only as the result of a triggering event. They define a trigger as "'a discrete event that represents culminating stimulus that may cause state instability leading to a high likelihood of state failure" (2010, 10), and list a variety of such triggers that include arbitrary arrests, armed attack, assassination, coups, elections, killings, protests, and secession (2010, 25). We see evidence of such triggers in the case studies presented in Chapter Five. For example, secession was a trigger in the case of the DRC's first collapse. Examples of armed attacks are found in the case of the DRC, Afghanistan, and Cambodia.

The work of Carment and colleagues is also focused on early warning systems. They similarly argue: "To effectively understand what effect a triggering event will have on a state it must be analyzed within the context of the state in which it occurs. Its history, ethnic tensions, economy, history of violence and other factors will all dictate how triggering events affect the index of state tension, and consequently the possibility of state failure" (Carment et al. 2006, 43). Again, we see the warning not to try a "one-size-fits-all" model. Carment (2006, 407) additionally argues that, no matter what the method of generating or gathering data, or the method of analyzing that data, we still do not have "a solid analytical base from which to generate good response strategies," nor a good track record in diagnosing failure ahead of time.[10] Carment (2003, 407) provides a "good news–bad news" summary, noting that the "disparate and often contending analytical approaches constitute a formidable and potentially useful tool-kit for risk assessment and early warning. However, there is a large and very real analytical gap between academics and practitioners on how to develop and use early warning techniques and methodologies."

We believe that through the analyses in the previous chapters, we have presented a solid, and parsimonious, list of basic causal factors for state collapse. We have outlined how such causal factors may diffuse in the wake of state collapse, thus presenting an outlook for the consequences of state failure. It is noteworthy that only a few states collapse more than once, which provides both some insights into the more pernicious sorts of collapse (recovery from which is harder to sustain) as well as presenting questions and challenges that the international community must continue to grapple with and address. We have also proposed a set of factors that appear to inhibit both the diffusion and reinforcement of collapse, and have traced the ways in which they appear to work in distinguishing double-collapse states from matching single-collapse cases. In so doing, we have seen under what conditions different mechanisms and proposed policies appear to work and when they are unsuccessful. We have also seen the impact of different types of triggers when conditions make states "ready" or "vulnerable" to collapse. Especially in looking at early warning approaches to state failure do we see the utility of studying state weakness or fragility. But here we also run headlong into the complexities of economic development, as well as political and institutional weakness and instability.

8 Conclusion

GENERAL OVERVIEW

We ended Chapter Seven noting the complexities of politics, institutions, and economic development, and how dealing with such complexities bedevils all those who try to formulate policy regarding "state failure." One central purpose of this book has been to illuminate a number of such complexities and, in turn, possible ways to deal with them. In Chapters One and Two, we presented a set of issues regarding the nature and study of state failure. These included problems with *cumulation* in results and difficulties in developing effective policy. In large part both problems stemmed from scholars and practitioners addressing different aspects of state failure, and asking different questions for different purposes. These were all caught up in a web of incomplete or opaque conceptualization of state failure—including both the intension and extension of the concept, as well as definition, and operationalization/measurement. And, drawing upon the earlier logic of inquiry work of Most and Starr (1989), we pointed out how these issues affected the quality of the research designs of studies concerned with state failure.

Various approaches to state failure have looked at it as weakness, fragility, instability, or collapse. Each of these characterizations has been shown to be of interest, as they all highlight different dimensions or "faces" of state failure, asking different questions about different processes involved. In this book we too have looked at different processes and questions: What have scholars meant by state failure? Is it an endpoint or a process? What are key causal factors in the occurrence of state failure? What are the factors involved in the duration of state failure or recovery from state failure? What factors are involved in the recurrence of failure in any single state? And what factors are involved in the spread or diffusion of state failure and its effects? Thus, we have been concerned with both the causes and consequences of state failure.

For key questions we have argued that it is best to study state failure as an endpoint. We selected an indicator of state collapse using the –77 code from the POLITY data set. Analyses in Chapters Three, Four, and Six were carried out using this conception and operationalization of state failure in large-N empirical models of the determinants, duration, and consequences of state collapse. However, with recurrence we were faced with a small number of cases and complex combinations of possible causal factors. Thus, in Chapter Five we used a design of matched case studies to deal with a classic example of the small-N/large-V problem. This type of approach was carried over to Chapter Seven, which addressed a range of policy proposals. In both cases, we were interested in *why* failure did not recur or *how* failure might be avoided or shortened; these questions could also help us return in Chapter Six to the question of why state failure itself was not found to diffuse. In both Chapters Five and Seven we addressed the complexities noted above (especially *causal* complexity), and argued that a "one-size-fits-all" solution to the prevention of either a first or subsequent collapse, recovery from collapse, or spread of state failure was not appropriate or feasible.

In each of the chapters that presented empirical analyses of state failure—Chapter Three through Chapter Six—we returned to our introductory chapters to support our earlier arguments with empirical evidence, and highlight the theory and research design difficulties we had raised. We want to stress that this project also supports the utility of multimethod research noted in Chapter One. The juxtaposition of a set of eight small-scale process tracing case studies in Chapter Five to the quantitative analyses in Chapters Three, Four, and Six allowed us to look more closely into the features that the variables used in the quantitative chapters were used to represent, and to see if the theoretical links proposed for the inclusion of those variables in our analyses held. The combination of analytical approaches was necessary for the presentation and evaluation of policy recommendations presented in Chapter Seven.

In sum, we have tried to meet the causal complexity of state failure and the many questions it raises with a set of analyses that cross multiple boundaries. We see this approach as a strength of our study, and one of its major contributions. In this first cut at a set of complex questions about state failure, we have crossed methodological boundaries—including quantitative and qualitative data as well as analytic techniques. We have crossed boundaries between basic research and policy. Perhaps more broadly, we have set the basic conceptualization of state failure and our broad approach within a context that crosses the subfields of International Relations and Comparative Politics, and thus levels of analysis as well. We have cut across two central areas of international relations, the study of conflict processes and the study of international/comparative political economy. In so doing, we think we have made a number of important contributions to the study of state failure.

SO WHAT? SOME PROMINENT FINDINGS

One thing is clear from our analyses: major causal factors for state failure found in the literature and employed in Chapter Three do reveal themselves to be important in the collapse or failure of states. High levels of democracy and high levels of wealth do indeed reduce the probability of state collapse. In addition, the democratic effect is curvilinear, which is to say that high levels of autocracy also reduce the probability of collapse, with the relatively unstable anocratic states the most liable to state failure. Civil war is a major contributor (perhaps *the* major causal factor) to the occurrence of state failure. While internationalized civil war is a major factor in state collapse, interstate war itself was found to have a relatively minor contribution, on par with unrest. This is especially so since the end of the Cold War. Indeed, the effects of interstate war were found to be relatively minor throughout our other analyses, with no effect on duration and little in the way of diffusion effects when looking at our entire time period. Other measures of internal conflict—unrest and instability—contributed to the increased probability of collapse, and also showed up in the contagion effects of spreading from collapsed states to states sharing contiguous borders. Regarding diffusion, higher levels of democracy and international interaction appeared to reduce the diffusion of unrest but not instability.

An important goal of this project has been to highlight that the effects of various factors are not identical with respect to different aspects of state failure. For instance, when evaluating the duration of collapse, high levels of democracy or wealth do not seem to have discernible effects. The analysis of duration and recovery introduced the dimension of economic openness and the importance of states being engaged with the world system as factors in reducing the length of time for which a state remained failed or collapsed. Economic openness and membership in economic and political international organizations were not found to be important to the cause of collapse, but were important in reducing the duration of collapse, preventing the recurrence of collapse, and in the failure of state collapse itself to spread. The central message to take away from these analyses is that different variables or factors have different levels of impact depending on the aspect of state failure under investigation (with some very large difference and some that are more nuanced).

Some of the most important of such findings are in Chapter Six on diffusion. While unrest and instability do have diffusion effects in contiguous neighbors, civil war exhibits the strongest effects on both contiguous neighbors and the failed state's near region. But while civil war exhibits the strongest diffusion effects, *state failure itself does not diffuse.* State failure itself does not lead to more failure in the same country (recurrence/reinforcement, as noted in Chapter Five); nor does it lead to more failure/collapse in other countries (spatial diffusion, in Chapter Six). Our findings on the importance of civil war for some questions, along with the finding that collapse itself does not diffuse, have consequences for the policy analysis in Chapter Seven, especially: *Why* does collapse not spread, and *how* can both of these effects exist? The latter question is important to those who define state failure by the presence of civil war. But given the role we find for civil war as a cause of collapse, and the strong nature of its diffusion, the fact that collapse itself does not diffuse means that we *cannot equate* state failure with civil war; one *does not* equal the other. Our discussion and research design warnings in Chapter Two are justified and supported by these results.

Thus we can assert that a study of state failure must involve an attempt to assess multiple questions that surround and arise from this rare but salient phenomenon in global security. We have here made such an attempt in taking a multidimensional approach to the understanding of state collapse, and in evaluating not just its causes but also its end and domestic and regional impacts.

FINAL COMMENTS

State failure, like any other phenomenon of international politics, occurs within the globalized environment of the current international system. Thus its onset, termination, duration, recurrence, and consequences are inextricably bound up with what is going on in the rest of the world—specifically, the involvement of the international community with the failing/failed state. While we have discussed international intervention in Chapters Five and Seven (in the contexts of state failure recurrence and policy implications of our analyses), much is left to be examined regarding the role that international actors could play in affecting the course of state collapse. External intervention and state collapse have an intricate relationship, with the possibility of effective intervention at multiple levels of the process of failure. While we treat state failure as a definite and absolute collapse of state authority, our analyses of the determinants of failure (as well as the influences on its duration and recurrence) provide insights into the processes through which that endpoint is reached. For instance, although we are careful not to conflate failure with civil war (as some other studies have done), we demonstrate that civil wars are closely associated with state collapse. Moreover, economic factors—such as national income—play a role in various dimensions of state failure. Therefore, nuanced assessments of international involvement before collapse, and intervention after collapse, would yield valuable insights into the occurrence (and prevention) of this rare but important phenomenon in the global system. To this end, it would be useful for the literatures (and scholars) that focus on issues of intervention and state failure to find better ways to speak to each other.

Of particular importance might be scholarly efforts to broaden the conceptualization of intervention through expanding the range of actors who could (or do) intervene in states and societies to lower the probability of collapse, reduce the length of time before a state can recover from failure, or diminish the likelihood of recurrent failure. For instance, instead of limiting our attention to intervention efforts by the United Nations and regional institutions, we could turn to how private entities—such as multinational corporations—play (or might play) a role in keeping states from collapsing: specifically, how that role could be better managed to have a positive influence on fragile states with high risks of failure, rather than merely subjecting these societies to the pernicious effects of the "dark side of globalization." Given the evidence that we find regarding the significant effects of various indicators of development on state failure, and the relationship that exists between multinational corporations and various aspects of development, this line of research could lead to a much more thorough understanding of how—and what forms of—international involvement can have the best (that is, most mitigating) impact on state collapse. In the absence of extant large-scale analyses, we are not in a position to assert whether the involvement of/with private entities would benefit a weak or failing state; we merely point to it as a future direction for further investigation of the concept and phenomenon of state failure.

What we can indeed deduce from the analyses we have conducted is that the study of state failure involves a complex and contested concept, with multiple dimensions and multiple meanings to different analysts. The study of a range of questions about state failure highlights the core issues of science—and the need for a community of scholars and researchers who bring different theories, hypotheses, approaches, and methods to their analyses. Different theoretical frameworks and approaches, as well as different case selection, data sources, methods of data collection, and methods of data analysis, will all be necessary for a full description, understanding, and policy response to state failure. The central issue *is not* to demand that all researchers ask the same questions or study those questions in the same way. What we have tried to do in this book is to provide the "research triad" of theory, logic, and research design called for by Most and Starr (1989), which was useful both for our own approach to state failure, and for facilitating the integration of knowledge about state failure from the work of multiple analysts. In this way we have followed in the foot-steps of Most and Starr (1989) by highlighting the impediments to cumulation and providing some guidance about how to avoid them and how to advance our general progress in understanding and dealing with state failure. This will not be a quick or easy task. This book is far from the final word on state failure, or an endpoint in its study. However, we hope that it has made a significant contribution to the continuing journey that the study of state failure requires.

Reference Matter

Notes

CHAPTER 1

1. Even more than twenty years after Rosenau's (1990) path-breaking treatment of "turbulence."

2. As noted by Murph-Schwarzer (2011), human security gained international attention following its inclusion and discussion in the UN's *Human Development Report* (*UNHDR*) in 1994. That report lists seven aspects of human security: economic security, food security, health security, environmental security, personal security, community security, and political security. Also included was a dual foundation of both "freedom from want" and "freedom from fear." The UN Development Programme has argued that the security of the individual is the building block for the security of the state. However, "human security" has much the same problems with definition and operationalization that we will discuss in regard to "state failure" (see Murph-Schwarzer 2011).

3. Article 2(4) of the UN Charter states: "All Members shall refrain in their international relations from the threat or use of force against the territorial integrity or political independence of any state, or in any other manner inconsistent with the Purposes of the United Nations."

CHAPTER 2

1. Langford (1999, 64), among others, agrees that many of these definitions are "vague" and not very helpful.

2. For example, definitions offered by the UK Department for International Development (DFID), The World Bank, the Fund for Peace, and the Political Instability Task Force. See also Patrick (2006), and Rotberg (2003) for other overviews of differing definitions, dimensions, and categories, such as strong, weak, failed, or collapsed states (Rotberg's continuum).

3. For example, Langford (1999, 59) observes: "State failure is a complex, multifac-

eted phenomenon that defies conventional methods of peacekeeping, peacemaking, and peacebuilding, and challenges the standard conceptual and operational frameworks within which international relations theorists and practitioners function."

4. The study of failed states appears to be an area that fits very well with "nice laws." Most and Starr note (1989, 18): "We argue that general propositions or 'laws' will miss important processes and relationships that occur in various subsystems, subgroups, or more limited, context-specific sets of actors or patterns of interaction."

5. What is now the Political Instability Task Force (PITF) appears not to fall into this trap.

6. Low-Income Countries Under Stress.

7. See http://web.worldbank.org/WBSITE/EXTERNAL/PROJECTS/STRATEGIES/

8. See www.brettonwoodsproject.org/art-542375.

9. For example, the World Justice Project provides four universal principles that embody the rule of law: (1) the government and its officials and agents are accountable under the law; (2) the laws are clear, publicized, stable, and fair, and protect fundamental rights including the security of persons and property; (3) access to justice is provided by competent, independent, and ethical advocates and neutrals who are of sufficient number, have adequate resources, and reflect the makeup of the communities they serve; and (4) the process by which the laws are enacted, administered, and enforced is accessible, fair, and efficient.

10. Rummel has also used the term "mortacracy" for "a regime that commits mass democide, such as did Nazi Germany, the Soviet Union, communist China, and Pol Pot's Cambodia, among others," including both the intentional deaths counted in democide and the unintentional deaths that result from their policies. Note that these examples are not failed states, but rather governments well in control of their territory and people whose goal is to reduce or erase a specific ethnic or political group. This occurred in Cambodia, but Saddam Hussein's Iraq as well, and going further back for an example, Stalin's policy toward the kulaks or Mao and the Cultural Revolution.

11. This section draws heavily on Starr (2008b).

12. However, it is important to note the critique of the POLITY data set out by Fearon and Laitin (2009, 25). They advise the PITF to investigate creating "clearer coding rules" for the –77 code representing "political interregnum" as well as specifying operational criteria for "collapse." They note: "The Polity manual defines –77 as 'a collapse of central authority.' Zaire in 1998 is the perfect example, inasmuch as there was such anarchy that any score between –10 and +10 would not have reflected the reality of lawlessness. But there are cases of –77 scores where there have been coup attempts, yet the political center remained in control over the governing apparatus," such as in Afghanistan in 1978.

13. While some scholars of state failure stress civil war, and come close to equating failure with civil war, in their analysis of the POLITY data set for the PITF Fearon and

Laitin (2009, 27) conclude: "[It] is clear that –77 is not entirely, or by definition, a coding of civil war, since there are –77's in the data in which there is clearly no civil war occurring (though such cases are relatively rare)." They come to this conclusion even after identifying "substantial violence" as one of the key criteria for being coded –77.

14. We selected this time frame to take best advantage of the time periods covered by the data collected across the various indexes. This is merely illustrative; there is no reason to believe that using longer time frames or more recent data would be more or less consistent across measures.

CHAPTER 3

1. Fazal (2004) examines the causes of "state death," which is defined as loss of sovereignty to another state resulting from conquest, colonization, or prolonged occupation. This conceptualization of state demise is more consistent with the POLITY code of –66, which denotes foreign occupation. We, on the other hand, examine factors associated with collapse of a state's central authority, irrespective of foreign invasion.

2. There is significant empirical evidence that reveals a negative relationship between democracy and dyadic conflict (for example, Reiter and Stam 1998; Russett 1993) as well as civil wars (for example, Hegre et al. 2001; Elbadawi and Sambanis 2002). Hence it may be expected that higher levels of democracy mitigate the influence of civil and interstate conflict on state failure. However, we evaluate the direct effect of regime type on state failure rather than its indirect effect through armed conflict.

3. Regarding the analytic distinction between civil war for control of government and secession, see, for example, Buhaug and Gates (2002), or Buhaug and Rød (2006).

4. See, for example, Kalyvas (2001) for arguments (and other literature) supporting the role and impact of ethnic/communal factors in the causes and consequences of civil war, especially in distinction from the work of others such as Fearon and Laitin (2003) and Collier and Hoeffler (2004), who find little impact for measures of ethnic factors.

5. For example, see Iqbal and Zorn (2007) for a discussion of the mitigating effect of Cold War influences on civil war and refugee flows.

6. POLITY guidelines suggest converting the POLITY score country-years with –77 to zero. To avoid endogeneity resulting from the nature of our dependent variable, we linearly interpolate the POLITY score for these years.

7. Because of missing data on some variables, the actual analysis starts from 1952.

8. This is consistent with the arguments of Bueno de Mesquita et al. (2003) concerning the effects of war on the "survival" of state leaders (rather than the collapse of governments or states).

CHAPTER 4

1. Somalia's government collapsed in 1991, and it was still a failed state in 2011, when the POLITY data were most recently updated. Because Somalia remained failed in the

year in which our data set ends, it is censored from our empirical analysis. It is, however, noteworthy that this collapse has lasted more than eighteen years.

2. According to the POLITY IV *Dataset Users' Manual* (17–18): "A '-77' code for the POLITY component variables indicates periods of 'interregnum,' during which there is a complete collapse of central political authority . . . . Interregnal periods are equated with the collapse, or failure, of central state authority, whether or not that failure is followed by a radical transformation, or revolution, in the mode of governance."

3. Because of our limited number of observations—only twenty-seven failures between 1960 and 2010—we limit our analysis to bivariate methods. As a result, these analyses are necessarily only suggestive. Additional data would be necessary to examine the marginal effect of state failure in a full multivariate context.

CHAPTER 5

1. We follow this strategy to avoid the problems found in some studies that include inordinately large numbers of possibly causal variables. Our goal throughout the present study is to be parsimonious (and much more theoretical) in our statistical analyses/ overviews, but look for finer-grained nuances in the case studies. Digging into areas of possible difference in the cases to follow will also note some specific components of the major factors used in the statistical analyses (but were not included in those analyses).

2. Note that Haiti in 2010 also was a close match to Afghanistan in 1978. However, Haiti was dropped from the matching exercise because it was the only case in the relevant list of –77 coded countries in which the governmental collapse could be directly attributed to a natural disaster. See Omelicheva (2011) on natural disasters as "triggers" of political instability.

3. Regarding duration, there is a slight indication that longer periods of failure will make it somewhat more difficult to avoid recurrence. While two of the double-failures failed for only a year or less (coded –77 for one year only), the other two—DRC and Ivory Coast—were failed for five years. Note that *only five* of the other eighteen single-failure cases had failure durations of five years or greater (Cyprus, Liberia, Somalia, Lebanon, and Laos). For the matched cases, only the Solomon Islands lasted more than a year (three years).

4. Note that this goes beyond Rotberg's observation (2003, 5) that "[in] contrast to strong states, failed states cannot control their borders. They lose authority over sections of territory." This would apply to any "failed" state—but does not take into account differing magnitudes of opportunity their borders provide, either in the numbers of neighbors or ease of interaction (if that had an effect).

5. Correlates of War Project, http://www.correlatesofwar.org/. CIOTOT data were gathered for 1950 through the 1997 period; thus there are no data for the Ivory Coast and the Solomon Islands.

6. The Freedom House classifications for Guinea-Bissau and Uganda matched those

of POLITY, with Partly Free (PF) ratings. However, Freedom House was more negative for Cambodia, rating it NF; and more negative for the Solomon Islands rating it PF (rather than Free).

7. Note that Powell and Wiegand (2010, 129) in their investigation of legal systems and territorial dispute resolution, observe that "states use their domestic legal systems to provide them with clues about the most trustworthy ways to settle disputes."

8. The judicial independence data were kindly provided by Randazzo.

9. While there are data for several other variables for the Ivory Coast–Solomon Islands dyad, none differentiate the two, or are in the proposed direction: for example, per capita health expenditures, foreign direct investment (FDI) net inflow, or annual percentage of GDP growth.

10. For example: the Penn World Tables variable "rgdpl" (PPP converted GDP per capita at 2005 constant prices) is almost twice as high for Afghanistan as for its matched single-failure case, Guinea-Bissau, while the figure for the DRC is 30 percent higher than its matched case, Cambodia.

11. Note that while much of the economic data that could be used for comparisons between the double-failure and their single-failure matched cases are not available for the double-failures at the time of their first failure, or, when they are, missing data for our specific cases limits our analyses, many such measures of absolute wealth or income do not show much difference (in either direction) when comparing the cases. For other variables, there is no consistency in comparing the double- and single-failures. Although there are data for some of the cases, we have found no impact regarding:

– FDI
– IBRD loans and IDA credits
– inflation
– income share held by the lowest 20 percent
– population growth
– literacy rates
– World Bank governance measures such as political stability and control of corruption.

12. Other analyses lead them to conclude that "[e]mpirical tests show that governments with access to revenue sources that require few labor inputs by the citizens, such as natural resource rents or foreign aid, reduce the provision of public goods and increase the odds of increased authoritarianism in the face of revolutionary pressures" (Bueno de Mesquita and Smith 2009b, 167).

13. We wish to thank Girod for supplying the data for our cases.

14. Material for the following case studies was drawn from a number of sources: POLITY IV Country Reports, the CIA World Factbook, the U.S. State Department Background Notes, Lexis/Nexis searches, the "Newsbank Access World News" database, Kees-

ing's Record of World Events, and Keesing's Archives. We would like to acknowledge the work of graduate assistants at Penn State University, and at the University of South Carolina, especially that of Ashley Murph-Schwarzer; also South Carolina undergraduate students Warren Durrett and Alexander Severson (as a South Carolina Magellan Scholar).

15. For example, there was the 1975 rebellion in Panjshir Province by the Jaimat Islamic Party. When defeated, the insurgents fled to a friendly Pakistan.

16. UNGOMAP's mandate was to monitor (1) noninterference and nonintervention by the parties in each other's affairs; (2) the withdrawal of Soviet troops from Afghanistan; and (3) the voluntary return of refugees. Having deemed these aims accomplished, UNGOMAP ceased operations in March 1990.

17. See the document at www.usip.org/files/file/resources/collections/peace_agreements/gb_11011998.pdf.

18. See www.un.org/depts/DPKO/Missions/onuc.htm>.

19. The Paris Agreement (October 28, 1991) was signed by the Cambodian government and FUNINPEC (the royalist political party) and the KPNLF (Khmer People's Liberation Front).

20. See www.un.org/en/peacekeeping/missions/past/untac.htm.

21. "Museveni Sworn in as President," The Times, January 30, 1986.

22. The rebels were initially known as the Cote d'Ivoire Patriotic Movement (MPCI) but later were called the New Forces.

23. The UN mandate included: monitoring of the cessation of hostilities and movements of armed group; disarmament, demobilization, reintegration, repatriation, and resettlement; disarmament and dismantling of militias; operations of identification of the population and registration of voters; reform of the security sector; protection of UN personnel, institutions, and civilians; monitoring of the arms embargo; support for humanitarian assistance; support for the redeployment of state administration; support for the organization of open, free, fair, and transparent elections; assistance in the field of human rights; public information; and law and order

24. Note that Fearon and Laitin (2009, 21–22) argue that civil war tends to be more likely in the year following a national election in anocratic states—an observation that seems apt in the case of the Ivory Coast.

25. See "IMF Delegation Finds Little Improvement in Solomon Islands," SIBC website (www.sibconline.com.sb/).

26. See www.ramsi.org/about/history.html.

27. Relating to failed states, this mechanism would be considered by a number of Western governments such as the United States, the UK, and Canada as a method of "stabilization." As Blair and Fitz-Gerald (2009, 3) note: "Each national approach makes the link between the requirement for stabilisation interventions in places where host

governments are weak or have lost the capacity to govern effectively, thus stressing the threat posed by instability and fragility."

28. The findings of these studies are reinforced by Oh's study of the termination of enduring rivalries: "The ultimate goal of studying rivalry termination is to find an answer to how we can successfully end contemporary rivalries. In this study, this is a matter of forming rivalry peace agreements and building an effective post-agreement implementation process" (Oh 2012, 96).

CHAPTER 6

1. An earlier version of the analysis in this chapter can be found in Iqbal and Starr (2008).

2. For example, see Salehyan and Gleditsch (2006) for a discussion of the regional clustering of civil war and the effects of refugee flows as one important factor in the diffusion of civil conflict. Note also the debate in the analysis of civil war over the effects of ethnicity; see Fearon and Laitin (2003) or Elbadawi and Sambanis (2000) for results that minimize the effects of ethnicity on civil war.

3. The Civil War variable contains all conflicts designated Type 3 in the PRIO Dataset on Armed Conflict. These are described as internal armed conflicts, and range in intensity from minor (with twenty-five battle deaths in a conflict) to intense (one thousand battle deaths in a given country-year).

4. All Type 2 conflicts (interstate armed conflict) in the PRIO Dataset on Armed Conflict.

5. Collier and Hoeffler (for example, 2004) have shown that low national income is a major factor in the occurrence of civil war. Thus, while a variety of possible economic measures could be used, we have opted for more parsimony, and included only national income and economic openness.

6. We chose to lag independent variables one year, as this provides us with the most rigorous test of our hypotheses regarding diffusion and contagion of the consequences of state failure; the one-year lag reflects the "minimum incubation period" for the spread of the effects of state collapse. We expect longer lags to strengthen our findings.

7. We estimated the models using both random effects and fixed effects approaches, and the two approaches yielded substantively similar results. Under these circumstances, random effects models have the virtue of being more efficient, as well as preserving information from observations that fixed effects models must necessarily exclude (Hsiao 2002). Alternative approaches to analyzing diffusion processes may include spatial lag and spatial error models. However, models for spatially referenced panel data (see, for example, Franzese and Hays 2007) are in their infancy, and we leave the use of those models for future work on the effects of state collapse.

8. Norman Alcock's *The War Disease* (1972) not only employs a similar epidemiological perspective but also includes a model of how and why the "disease" spreads.

CHAPTER 7

1. Hamre and Sullivan (2002, 89) note: "The definition of the term, as used in this article, includes providing and enhancing not only social and economic well-being and governance and the rule of law but also other elements of justice and reconciliation and, very centrally, security."

2. Bueno de Mesquita and Smith (2009a, 36) note that the people in autocracies receiving aid are harmed in two ways: they get policies they would rather not have; and "the aid helps their autocratic incumbent leadership survive and continue to pursue unpopular policies in the future. Thus, citizens in the recipient state get 'bad policies' and 'bad leaders.'" Using OECD bilateral aid transfers between 1960 and 2001, they provide empirical support for the predictions generated by the political survival model as presented here and elsewhere (for example, Bueno de Mesquita and Smith 2007; Smith 2008).

3. Hamre and Sullivan (2002, 92) similarly argue: "Primary responsibility and leadership roles must rest with the people of the country in question. At the same time, the local population cannot be left to solve its own problems. The international community can play a critical role in providing assistance."

4. Note that Daxecker and Prins try to predict which states will have a piracy incident (yes/no rather than the frequency of incidents). Note also that their results (2011, 18) show that "state fragility" is a better predictor of the occurrence or nonoccurrence of incidents (of actual attacks/hijackings) than any other single variable in all their models.

5. A similar debate can be found in the Rule of Law literature as how best to create constitutions, legal systems, as well as effective and stable institutions, norms, and practices.

6. See, for example, Diehl's "taxonomy of peacekeeping missions" (2008, 15): traditional peacekeeping; observation; collective enforcement; election supervision; humanitarian assistance during conflict; state/nation building; pacification; preventive deployment; arms control verification; protective services; and intervention in support of democracy. Note that "pacification" and "protective services" best match up with Mueller's idea of "policing."

7. However, we must keep in mind that Chapter Five was focused on reinforcement, or the repeated failure of states, not on the initial collapse.

8. Hamre and Sullivan (2002) present a set of policy options, one of which would be to "quarantine" the failed state—which would also be one way of preventing or limiting diffusion.

9. The eight models are from the following:

- Conflict Analysis Framework (CAF)—World Bank
- Conflict Analysis for Project Planning and Management (GTZ)
- UNDP Conflict-Related Development Analysis

- Conflict Assessment System Tool (CAST)—Fund for Peace
- Stability Assessment Framework: Designing Integrated Responses for Security, Governance and Development (Clingendael Institute)
- An Early Warning Approach to Conflict and Instability Approach: The Fuzzy Analysis of Statistical Evidence (FASE) model. (U.S. Army Center for Army Analysis)
- FAST Analytical Framework
- Conflict Indicators for Foreign Policy (CIFP) (Carleton University)

10. See Carment (2003) for a good review of the earlier causes of state failure literature, as well as an overview of different approaches and methodologies to forecasting models (for example, 2003, 419), especially Gupta (1997).

References

Adcock, Robert, and David Collier. 2001. "Measurement Validity: A Shared Standard for Qualitative and Quantitative Research." *American Political Science Review* 95 (3): 529–46.

Ades, Albert., and R. Di Tella. 1999. "Rents, Competition, and Corruption." *American Economic Review* 89 (4): 982–93.

Alcock, Norman Z. 1972. *The War Disease*. Ontario: CPRI Press.

Backer, David A., and Paul K. Huth. 2014. "The Peace and Conflict Instability Ledger: Ranking States on Future Risks." In *Peace and Conflict 2014*, edited by David A. Backer, Jonathan Wilkenfeld, and Paul K. Huth, pp. 4–17. Boulder, CO: Paradigm Publishers.

Banks, Arthur S., and Kenneth A. Wilson. 2012. Cross-National Time-Series Data Archive. Databanks International. Jerusalem, Israel. See http://www.databanksinternational.com.

Bates, Robert H. 2008a. "The Logic of State Failure: Learning from Late-Century Africa." *Conflict Management and Peace Science* 25 (4): 297–314.

———. 2008b. *When Things Fell Apart: State Failure in Late-Century Africa*. Cambridge: Cambridge University Press.

Beardsley, Kyle. 2011. "Peacekeeping and the Contagion of Armed Conflict." *Journal of Politics* 73 (4): 1051–64.

Beck, Neal, Kristian Gleditsch, and Kyle Beardsley. 2006. "Space Is More than Geography: Using Spatial Econometrics in the Study of Political Economy." *International Studies Quarterly* 50 (1): 27–44.

Blair, Stephanie, and Ann Fitz-Gerald. 2009. "Stabilisation and Stability Operations: A Literature Review." Centre for Security Sector Management, Cranfield University, England, June 2009.

Bobrow, Davis. 1972. *International Relations, New Approaches*. New York: Free Press.

Box-Steffensmeier, Janet, Dan Reiter, and Christopher Zorn. 2003. "Nonproportional

Hazards and Event History Analysis in International Relations." *Journal of Conflict Resolution* 47 (1): 33–53.

Braumoeller, Bear. 2003. "Causal Complexity and the Study of Politics." *Political Analysis* 11 (3): 209–33.

Bueno de Mesquita, Bruce, and Alastair Smith. 2007. "Foreign Aid and Policy Concessions." *Journal of Conflict Resolution* 51 (2): 251–84.

———. 2009a. "A Political Economy of Aid." *International Organization* 63 (2): 309–40.

———. 2009b. "Institutional Survival and Endogenous Institutional Change." *Comparative Political Studies* 42 (2): 167–97.

Bueno de Mesquita, Bruce, Alastair Smith, Randolph Siverson, and James Morrow. 2003. *The Logic of Political Survival.* Cambridge, MA: MIT Press.

Buhaug, Halvard, and Scott Gates. 2002. "The Geography of Civil War." *Journal of Peace Research* 39 (4): 417–33.

Buhaug, Halvard, and Jan Ketil Rød. 2006. "Local Determinants of African Civil Wars, 1970–2001." *Political Geography* 25 (3): 315–25.

Call, Charles T. 2011. "Beyond the Failed State: Toward Conceptual Alternatives." *European Journal of International Relations* 17 (2): 303–26

Carment, David. 2006. "Assessing State Failure: Implications for Theory and Policy." *Third World Quarterly* 24: 407–27.

Carment, David, Souleima El-Achkar, Stewart Prest, and Yiagadeesen Samy. "The 2006 Country Indicators for Foreign Policy: Opportunities and Challenges for Canada." *Canadian Foreign Policy* 13: 1–35.

Carment, David, Souleima El-Achkar, John Gazo, Stewart Prest, and Yiagadeesen Samy. 2006. "Failed and Fragile States: A Briefing Note to the Canadian Government." Country Indicators for Foreign Policy, Failed and Fragile States Project, Carleton University.

Carment, David, Yiagadeesen Samy, and Stewart Prest. 2008. "State Fragility and Implications for Aid Allocation: An Empirical Analysis." *Conflict Management and Peace Science* 25 (4): 349–73.

Chauvet, Lisa, and Paul Collier. 2008. "What Are the Preconditions for Turnarounds in Failing States?" *Conflict Management and Peace Science* 25 (4): 332–48.

Chauvet, Lisa. et al. 2006. *The Cost of Failing States and the Limits to Sovereignty.* United Nations University, World Institute for Development Economics Research Working Paper.

Chopra, Jarat. 1996. "The Space of Peace-Maintenance." *Political Geography* 15: 335–57.

———. 1998. "Introducing Peace-Maintenance." *Global Governance* 4: 1–18.

Collier, David, and Steven Levitsky. 1997. "Democracy with Adjectives: Conceptual Innovation in Comparative Research." *World Politics* 49 (3): 430–51.

Collier, Paul, and Anke Hoeffler. 2004. "Greed and Grievance in Civil War." *Oxford Economic Papers* 56 (4): 563–95.

Correlates of War Project. 2011. "State System Membership List, v2011." See http://correlatesofwar.org.

Daxecker, Ursula, and Brandon Prins. 2011. "The New Barbary Wars: Forecasting Maritime Piracy." Paper presented at the 2011 Annual Meeting of the International Studies Association, San Diego, CA, April 1–4.

De Soysa, Indra, and Hanne Fjelde. 2010. "Is the Hidden Hand an Iron Fist? Capitalism and Civil Peace, 1970–2005." *Journal of Peace Research* 47 (3): 287–98.

Diehl, Paul. 2008. *Peace Operations*. Cambridge: Polity Press.

The Economist, March 5, 2005.

Eizenstat, Stuart E., John Edward Porter, and Jeremy M. Weinstein. 2005. "Rebuilding Weak States." *Foreign Affairs* 84: 134–46.

Elbadawi, Ibrahim, and Nicholas Sambanis. 2000. "How Much War Will We See? Estimating the Incidence of Civil War in 161 Countries." Geneva: World Bank.

———. 2002. "How Much War Will We See? Explaining the Prevalence of Civil War." *Journal of Conflict Resolution* 46 (3): 307–34.

Englebert, Pierre, and Denis M. Tull. 2008. "Postconflict Reconstruction in Africa: Flawed Ideas about Failed States." *International Security* 32 (4): 106–39.

Esty, Daniel C., Jack A. Goldstone, Ted R. Gurr, Barbara Harff, Marc Levy, Geoffrey D. Dabelko, Pamela T. Surko, and Alan N. Unger. 1998. "State Failure Task Force Report: Phase II Findings." McLean, VA: Science Applications International Corporation (SAIC).

Eyerman, Joe. 1998. "Terrorism and Democratic States: Soft Targets or Accessible Systems." *International Interactions* 24 (2): 151–70.

Fazal, Tanisha M. 2004. "State Death in the International System." *International Organization* 58 (2): 311–44.

Fearon, James D., and David D. Laitin. 2003. "Ethnicity, Insurgency, and Civil War." *American Political Science Review* 97 (1): 75–90.

———. 2009. *Political Instability and Civil War Onset: Report on a Research Project for the Political Instability Task Force*. Stanford University.

Franck, Thomas M. 1985. "The Strategic Role of Legal Principles." In *The Falklands War: Lessons for Strategy, Diplomacy, and International Law*, edited by Alberto R. Coll and Anthony C. Arend, pp. 22–33. London: Unwin Hyman.

Franzese, Robert J., Jr., and Jude C. Hays. 2007. "Spatial-Econometric Models of Cross-Sectional Interdependence in Political-Science Panel and Time-Series-Cross-Section Data." *Political Analysis* 15 (2): 140–64.

Frohlich, Norman, and Joe A. Oppenheimer. 1970. "I Get By with a Little Help from My Friends." *World Politics* 23 (1): 104–20.

Fund for Peace. 2006. *Failed States Index*. Washington, DC: The Fund for Peace. See http://www.fundforpeace.org/programs/fsi/fsindex.php.

Gates, Robert M. 2010. "Helping Others Defend Themselves: The Future of US Security Assistance." *Foreign Affairs* 89 (3): 2–6.

Gibler, Douglas M., and Kirk A. Randazzo. 2011. "Testing the Effects of Independent Judiciaries on the Likelihood of Democratic Backsliding." *American Journal of Political Science* 55 (3): 696–709.

Girod, Desha. 2012. "Effective Foreign Aid following Civil War: The Nonstrategic-Desperation Hypothesis." *American Journal of Political Science* 56 (1): 188–201.

Gleditsch, Kristian Skrede. 2002a. *All International Politics Is Local: The Diffusion of Conflict, Integration, and Democratization.* Ann Arbor: University of Michigan Press.

———. 2002b. "Expanded Trade and GDP Data." *Journal of Conflict Resolution* 46 (5): 712–24.

Gleditsch, Kristian Skrede, and Michael D. Ward. 2000. "War and Peace in Space and Time: The Role of Democratization." *International Studies Quarterly* 44 (1): 1–29.

Gleditsch, Nils Petter, Peter Wallensteen, Mikael Eriksson, Margareta Sollenberg and Håvard Strand. (2002). "Armed Conflict 1946–2001: A New Dataset." *Journal of Peace Research* 39 (5): 615–37.

Goertz, Gary. 2005. *Social Science Concepts: A User's Guide.* Princeton: Princeton University Press.

Goldstone, Jack A. 2008. "Pathways to State Failure." *Conflict Management and Peace Science* 25 (4): 285–96.

Goldstone, Jack A., Ted Robert Gurr, Barbara Harff, Marc A. Levy, Monty G. Marshall, Robert H. Bates, David L. Epstein. et al. 2000. "State Failure Task Force Report: Phase III Findings." McLean, VA, Science Applications International Corporation (SAIC).

Grant, Thomas D. 2004. "Partition of Failed States: Impediments and Impulses." *Journal of Global Legal Studies* 11 (2): 51–82.

Gupta, Dipak. 1997. "An Early Warning about Forecasts: Oracle to Academics." In *Synergy in Early Warning Conference Proceedings*, edited by Susanne Schmeidl and Howard Adelman. Toronto, Canada, March 1997, 375–96.

Hales, Doug, and Jordan Miller. 2010. *Triggers of State Failure.* No. DRDC-TORONTO-CR-2008–054. CAE Professional Services Ottawa (Ontario).

Hampson, Fen Osler, Jean Daudelin, John B. Hay, Todd Martin, and Holly Reid. 2002. *Madness in the Multitude: Human Security and World Disorder.* Ontario, Canada: Oxford University Press.

Hamre, John J., and Gordon R. Sullivan. 2002. "Toward Postconflict Reconstruction." *Washington Quarterly* 25: 85–96.

Hartzell, Caroline, Matthew Hoddie, and Donald Rothchild. 2001. "Stabilizing the Peace after Civil War: An Investigation of Some Key Variables." *International Organization* 55 (1): 183–208.

Hegre, Havard, Tanja Ellingsen, Scott Gates, and Nils Petter Gleditsch. 2001. "Toward a Democratic Civil Peace? Democracy, Political Change, and Civil War, 1816–1992." *American Political Science Review* 95 (1): 33–48.

Helman, Gerald B., and Steven R. Ratner. 1992–93. "Saving Failed States." *Foreign Policy* 89: 3–20.

Hensel, Paul R., Sara McLaughlin Mitchell, and Thomas E. Sowers. 2006. "Conflict Management of Riparian Disputes." *Political Geography* 25 (4): 383–411.

Herbst, Jeffrey. 1996–97. "Responding to State Failure in Africa." *International Security* 21: 120–44.

Heston, Alan, Robert Summers, and Bettina Aten. 2011. "Penn World Table." Center for International Comparisons at the University of Pennsylvania (CICUP).

Hoeffler, Anke. 2010. "State Failure and Conflict Recurrence." In *Peace and Conflict 2010*, edited by J. Joseph Hewitt et al., pp. 65–78. Boulder, CO: Palgrave.

Hsiao, Cheng. 2002. *Analysis of Panel Data.* 2nd ed. New York: Cambridge University Press.

Huntington, Samuel P. 1991. *The Clash of Civilizations and the Remaking of World Order.* New York: Simon and Schuster.

Iqbal, Zaryab. 2006. "Health and Human Security: The Public Health Impact of Violent Conflict." *International Studies Quarterly* 50 (3): 631–49.

———. 2007. "The Geo-Politics of Forced Migration in Africa, 1992–2001." *Conflict Management and Peace Science* 24 (2): 105–19.

———. 2010. *War and the Health of Nations.* Stanford: Stanford University Press.

Iqbal, Zaryab, and Harvey Starr. 2008. "Bad Neighbors: Failed States and Their Consequences." *Conflict Management and Peace Science* 25 (4): 315–31.

Iqbal, Zaryab, and Christopher Zorn. 2007. "Civil War and Refugees in Post–Cold War Africa." *Civil Wars* 9 (2): 200–213.

Kalyvas, Stathis N. 2001. "'New' and 'Old' Civil Wars: A Valid Distinction?" *World Politics* 54 (October): 99–118.

Kaplan, Seth. 2010. "Re-Thinking State Building in a Failed State." *Washington Quarterly* 33: 81–97.

Karreth, Johannes, and Jaroslav Tir. 2013. "International Institutions and Civil War Prevention." *American Journal of Political Science* 75 (1): 96–109.

King, Gary, and Langche Zeng. 2001. "Improving Forecasts of State Failure." *World Politics* 53 (4): 623–58.

Kisangani, Emizet N. F., and Jeffrey Pickering. 2008. *Codebook: International Military Intervention 1989–2005.* Inter-University Consortium for Political and Social Research, University of Michigan, Ann Arbor.

Krasner, Stephen D. 2004. "Sharing Sovereignty." *International Security* 29 (2): 85–120.

Langford, Tonya. 1999. "Things Fall Apart: State Failure and the Politics of Intervention." *International Studies Review* 1 (1): 59–79.

Mack, Andrew. 2005. *The Human Security Report 2005: War and Peace in the 21st Century.* Oxford: Oxford University Press.

Marshall, Monty G., et al. 1999. "Memberships in Conventional International Organizations 1952–1997." Center for Systemic Peace, George Mason University.

Marshall, Monty G., and Benjamin R. Cole. 2009. *Global Report 2009: Conflict, Governance, and State Fragility*. Center for Systemic Peace, George Mason University.

Marshall, Monty G., and Keith Jaggers. 2011. "*POLITY IV Project:* Political Regime Characteristics and Transitions, 1800–2011." Integrated Network for Societal Conflict Research Program and Center for International Development and Conflict Management, University of Maryland.

Mattes, Michaela, and Burcu Savun. 2009. "Fostering Peace after Civil War: Commitment Problems and Agreement Design." *International Studies Quarterly* 53 (3): 737–59.

McGowan, Patrick J. 2006. "Coups and Conflict in West Africa, 1955–2004: Part II Empirical Findings." *Armed Forces and Society* 32 (2): 234–53.

Midlarsky, Manus. 1975. *On War*. New York: Free Press.

Morgan, Stephen L., and Christopher Winship. 2007. *Counterfactuals and Causal Inference: Methods and Principles for Social Research*. New York: Cambridge University Press.

Most, Benjamin A., and Harvey Starr. 1980. "Diffusion, Reinforcement, Geopolitics, and the Spread of War." *American Political Science Review* 74 (4): 932–46.

———. 1989. *Inquiry, Logic and International Politics*. Columbia: University of South Carolina Press.

———. 1990. "Theoretical and Logical Issues in the Study of International Diffusion." *Journal of Theoretical Politics* 2 (4): 391–412.

Mousseau, Michael. 2000. "Market Prosperity, Democratic Consolidation, and Democratic Peace." *Journal of Conflict Resolution* 44 (August): 472–507.

———. 2003. "The Nexus of Market Society, Liberal Preferences, and Democratic Peace: Interdisciplinary Theory and Evidence." *International Studies Quarterly* 47 (4): 483–510.

Mueller, John. 1989. *Retreat from Doomsday*. New York: Basic Books.

———. 1995. *Quiet Cataclysm: Reflections on the Recent Transformations of World Politics*. New York: HarperCollins.

———. 2003. "Policing the Remnants of War." *Journal of Peace Research* 40 (5): 507–18.

———. 2004. *The Remnants of War*. Ithaca, NY: Cornell University Press.

———. 2011. *War and Ideas: Selected Essays*. New York: Routledge.

Murdoch, James C., and Todd Sandler. 2002. "Civil Wars and Economic Growth: A Regional Comparison." *Defence and Peace Economics* 13 (6): 451–64.

Murph-Schwarzer, Ashley. 2011. "Human Security Disaggregated: A Theoretical Approach." Paper presented at the Annual Meeting of the Southern Political Science Association, New Orleans, LA, January 6–8.

Oh, Soonkun. 2012. "How Rivalries End: Understanding Dynamics of the Rivalry Termination Process." Ph.D. dissertation, University of South Carolina.

O'Loughlin, John, and Frank Witmer. 2005. "Taking 'Geography' Seriously: Disaggregating the Study of Civil Wars." Paper presented at the conference on "Disaggregating the Study of Civil War and Transnational Violence," University of California Institute of Global Conflict and Cooperation, La Jolla, March 6–8.

Olson, Mancur. 2000. *Power and Prosperity*. New York: Basic Books.

Omelicheva, Mariya Y. 2011. "Natural Disasters: Triggers of Political Instability?" *International Interactions* 37 (4): 441–65.

Patrick, Stewart. 2006. "Weak States and Global Threats: Factor Fiction?" *Washington Quarterly* 29 (2): 27–53.

Powell, Emilia J., and Krista E. Wiegand. 2010. "Legal Systems and Peaceful Attempts to Resolve Territorial Disputes." *Conflict Management and Peace Science* 27 (2): 129–51.

Ray, James Lee. 1998. "Does Democracy Cause Peace?" *Annual Review of Political Science* 1 (1): 27–46.

Reiter, Dan, and Allan C. Stam III. 1998. "Democracy, War Initiation, and Victory." *American Political Science Review* 92 (2): 377–89.

Rice, S. E., and Stewart Patrick. 2003. *Index of State Weakness in the Developing World*. Washington, DC: Brookings Institution.

Richardson, Henry I. III. 1996. "'Failed States,' Self-Determination, and Preventative Diplomacy: Colonialist Nostalgia and Democratic Expectations." *Temple International and Comparative Law Journal* 10: 1–78.

Rosenau, James N. 1990. *Turbulence in World Politics*. Princeton: Princeton University Press.

Rost, Nicolas, and J. Michael Greig. 2011. "Taking Matters into Their Own Hands: An Analysis of the Determinants of State-Conducted Peacekeeping in Civil Wars." *Journal of Peace Research* 48 (2): 171–84.

Rotberg, Robert I. 2002. "The New Nature of Nation-State Failure." *Washington Quarterly* 25 (3): 85–96.

———. 2003. "Failed States, Collapsed States, Weak States: Causes and Indicators." In *State Failure and State Weakness in a Time of Terror*, edited by R. I. Rotberg et al., pp. 1–25. Washington, DC: Brookings Institution Press.

Rummel, Rudolph J. 1994. *Death by Government: Genocide and Mass Murder in the Twentieth Century*. Piscataway: Transaction Publishers.

Russett, Bruce. 1993. *Grasping the Democratic Peace: Principles for a Post–Cold War World*. Princeton: Princeton University Press.

Russett, Bruce M., and Harvey Starr. 2000. "From Democratic Peace to Kantian Peace: Democracy and Conflict in the International System." In *Handbook of War Studies II*, edited by Manus Midlarsky, pp. 93–128. Ann Arbor: University of Michigan Press.

Salehyan, Idean, and Kristian S. Gleditsch. 2006. "Refugees and the Spread of Civil War." *International Organization* 60 (2): 335–66.

Sambanis, Nicholas. 2002. "A Review of Recent Advances and Future Directions in the Quantitative Literature on Civil War." *Defence and Peace Economics* 13 (3): 215–43.

Schultz, Kenneth A. 2010. "The Enforcement Problem in Coercive Bargaining: Interstate Conflict over Rebel Support in Civil Wars." *International Organization* 64 (2): 281–312.

Shaffer, Matt. 2012. "Economic Agreements, Intra-Agreement Conflict, and Policy Substitution." Paper presented at the Annual Meeting of the International Studies Association, San Diego, CA, April 1 4.

Simmons, Beth. 2002. "Capacity, Commitment, and Compliance: International Institutions and Territorial Disputes." *Journal of Conflict Resolution* 46 (6): 829–56.

Simmons, Beth, and Zachary Elkins. 2004. "The Globalization of Liberalization: Policy Diffusion in the International Political Economy." *American Political Science Review* 98 (1): 171–89.

Simon, Marc V., and Harvey Starr. 1996. "Extraction, Allocation, and the Rise and Decline of States." *Journal of Conflict Resolution* 40 (2): 272–97.

———. 2000. "Two-level Security Management and the Prospects for New Democracies: A Simulation Analysis." *International Studies Quarterly* 44 (3): 391–422.

Siverson, Randolph M., and Harvey Starr. 1991. *The Diffusion of War.* Ann Arbor: University of Michigan Press.

Smith, Alastair. 2008. "The Perils of Unearned Income." *Journal of Politics* 70 (3): 780–93.

Sobek, David. 2010. "Masters of Their Domains: The Role of State Capacity in Civil Wars." *Journal of Peace Research* 47 (3): 267–71.

Starr, Harvey. 1991. "Democratic Dominoes: Diffusion Approaches to the Spread of Democracy in the International System." *Journal of Conflict Resolution* 35 (2): 356–81.

———. 1994. "Revolution and War: Rethinking the Linkage between Internal and External Conflict." *Political Research Quarterly* 47 (2): 481–507.

———. 1997. *Anarchy, Order, and Integration: How to Manage Interdependence.* Ann Arbor: University of Michigan Press.

———. 2002. "Opportunity, Willingness and Geographic Information Systems: Reconceptualizing Borders in International Relations." *Political Geography* 21 (2): 243–26.

———. 2003. "The Power of Place and the Future of Spatial Analysis in the Study of Conflict." *Conflict Management and Peace Science* 20 (1): 1–20.

———. 2005. "Territory, Proximity, and Spatiality: The Geography of International Conflict." *International Studies* Review 7 (3): 387–406.

———, ed. 2006. *Approaches, Levels and Methods of Analysis in International Politics: Crossing Boundaries.* New York: Palgrave.

———, ed. 2008a. "Failed States." Special issue, *Conflict Management and Peace Science* 25 (4).

———. 2008b. "Introduction to the Special Issue on Failed States." *Conflict Management and Peace Science* 25 (4): 281–84.

———. 2009. "Borders, Ease of Interactions, Transactions and Cooperation: Tracking Integration in the EU across Waves of Expansion." Paper presented at the Annual North American Meeting of the Peace Science Society (International), Chapel Hill, NC, November 2009.

———. 2013. *On Geopolitics: Space, Place, and International Relations.* Boulder, CO: Paradigm Publishers.

Starr, Harvey, and Christina Lindborg. 2003. "Democratic Dominoes Revisited: The Hazards of Governmental Transitions, 1974–96." *Journal of Conflict Resolution* 47 (4): 490–519.

Starr, Harvey, and Benjamin A. Most. 1983. "Contagion and Border Effects on Contemporary African Conflict." *Comparative Political Studies* 16 (1): 92–117.

———. 1985. "The Forms and Processes of Diffusion: Research Update on Contagion in African Conflict." *Comparative Political Studies* 18 (2): 206–27.

Starr, Harvey, and G. Dale Thomas. 2005. "The Nature of Borders and Conflict: Revisiting Hypotheses on Territory and War." *International Studies Quarterly* 49 (1): 123–39.

Strand, Havard, Lars Wilhelmsen, and Nils Petter Gleditsch. 2004. *Armed Conflict Dataset Codebook, Version 3.0.* Oslo: International Peace Research Institute.

United Kingdom Department for International Development. 2005. *Why We Need to Work More Effectively in Fragile States.* London: Department for International Development.

United Nations Development Programme. 1994. *Human Development Report.* Oxford: Oxford University Press.

Van de Walle, Nicolas. 2004. "The Economic Correlates of State Failure: Taxes, Foreign Aid, and Policies." In *When States Fail: Causes and Consequences*, edited by Robert I. Rotberg, pp. 94–115. Princeton: Princeton University Press.

Vision of Humanity. 2008. See http://www.visionofhumanity.org/gpi-data/.

Wallerstein, Immanuel. 1974. *The Modern World System.* New York: Academic Press.

Walter, Barbara F. 2004. "Does Conflict Beget Conflict? Explaining Recurring Civil War." *Journal of Peace Research* 41 (3): 371–88.

Ward, Michael D., and Kristian S. Gleditsch. 1998. "Democratizing for Peace." *American Political Science Review* 92 (1): 51–61.

———. 2002. "Location, Location, Location: An MCMC Approach to Modeling the Spatial Context of War and Peace." *Political Analysis* 10 (3): 244–60.

Werner, Suzanne, David Davis, and Bruce Bueno de Mesquita. 2003. "Dissolving Boundaries: An Introduction." *International Studies Review* 5 (4): 1–7.

World Bank. 2002. *World Bank Group Work in Low-Income Countries under Stress.* Washington, DC: World Bank Group.

———. 2004. *Human Development Index.* Washington, DC: World Bank Group.

———. 2011. See http://web.worldbank.org.

Zacher, Mark. 2001. "The Territorial Integrity Norm: International Boundaries and the Use of Force." *International Organization* 55 (2): 215–50.

Index

Adcock, Robert, 21
Afghanistan: autocracy, 57, 66, 67; economic
   agreements, 56; ethnic divisions,
   67; history, 66–68; monarchy, 67;
   peacekeeping missions, 68, 112, 134n16;
   state failures, 51, 66–68, 80, 88; violent
   conflicts, 65
Africa: autocracies, 87; economic
   agreements, 56; foreign aid effectiveness,
   64; former colonies, 3, 71; study of
   failed states, 4. *See also* ECOWAS; *and
   individual countries*
Amin, Idi, 78, 79
Annan, Kofi, 7
Anocracies: civil wars in, 134n24; examples,
   58; governmental performance, 17;
   POLITY IV scores, 22; vulnerability to
   state failure, 32, 87. *See also* Regime types;
   and individual countries
Arab Spring, 92
Argentina, 6
Armed conflict, *see* Civil wars; Conflict;
   Interstate conflicts
Australia: Regional Assistance Mission to
   Solomon Islands, 84, 85–86, 112; South
   Pacific Regional Trade and Economic
   Cooperation Agreement, 56
Autocracies: in Africa, 87; foreign aid
   received, 109, 136n2; governmental
   performance, 17; vulnerability

to state failure, 29, 32, 37, 87. *See
   also* Regime types; *and individual
   countries*

Background concepts, 20, 21
Banks, Arthur S., 33, 43, 95
Bates, Robert H., 18, 87
Beardsley, Kyle, 88–89
Belgium, 71
Blair, Stephanie, 89, 111, 113
Bordering states: ease of interaction with,
   53–54, 54 (table); likelihood of state
   failure contagion, 90, 91, 94, 95, 96,
   99, 101 (table), 102–3, 124; number of
   contiguous, 52, 53, 54 (table), 66; salience,
   54, 54 (table). *See also* Diffusion of
   conflict
Bretton Woods Project, 16
Brookings Institution State Weakness Index,
   26
Bueno de Mesquita, Bruce, 25, 62, 63, 109–10,
   113
Businesses, multinational, 125

Call, Charles T., 5
Cambodia: anocracy, 58; autocracy,
   73, 74–75; economic agreements, 57;
   independence, 73; infant mortality rates,
   60; peacekeeping missions, 75, 114–15; Pol
   Pot regime, 60, 74–75; recovery from state

The authorized representative in the EU for product safety and compliance is:
Mare Nostrum Group
B.V Doelen 72
4831 GR Breda
The Netherlands

www.ingramcontent.com/pod-product-compliance
Lightning Source LLC
Chambersburg PA
CBHW030850270326
41928CB00008B/1309